8⁹⁵

THE OFFICIAL MIXER'S MANUAL

THE OFFICIAL MIXER'S MANUAL

THE STANDARD GUIDE FOR
PROFESSIONAL & AMATEUR BARTENDERS
THROUGHOUT THE WORLD

Patrick Gavin Duffy

REVISED AND ENLARGED BY

Robert Jay Misch

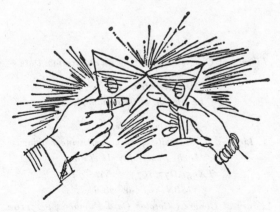

ILLUSTRATIONS BY REISIE LONETTE

DOUBLEDAY & COMPANY, INC.
GARDEN CITY, NEW YORK

Library of Congress Cataloging in Publication Data

Duffy, Patrick Gavin.
The official mixer's manual.

Includes index.
1. Liquors. 2. Cocktails. 3. Wine and wine making.
I. Misch, Robert Jay. II. Title.
TX951.D77 1975   641.8'74
ISBN 0-385-02328-6
Library of Congress Catalog Card Number 74–25119

CONTENTS

INTRODUCTION TO THE 1975 EDITION

How could they have picked a more suitable person to revise, redo, reorient, review and rewrite *The Official Mixer's Manual* than one, Robert Jay *Misch*. Misch was my father's name and his father's name and, I am told "Misch" in German means mix!

Mixing is a large part of the story of alcoholic beverages. Pay no attention to the self-appointed purist who declares, "I never touch mixed drinks." Rubbish. What does he drink then—wine? Well, he should know that all wine is a blend too—yes, even Château Lafite Rothschild has three or four different grapes in it. The cuvée of a decent Champagne is composed of twenty or thirty different wines. Cognac is normally blended of Grand Fine Champagnes, Fine Bois, Borderies and other brandies from demarcated areas of the Charente. And, of course, the snob is aware that Scotch is a blend of Highland and Lowland malts, Islays, Campbeltowns and grain Whiskies—just as Bourbon is a mix of a number of Whiskies and the blends, what their name implies, a blend of Whisky and neutral spirits or "light" Whisky.

But, there are good mixes and bad ones—and ones in between.

Prohibition was no help at all in the mixing department. One bathtub might have been all right and another could have been terrible. One bootlegger brought good stuff; another, a brew made from scrapings off the sides of ships. One speakeasy purveyed civilized drinks; another disguised the taste of rot-gut with liberal dollops of grenadine. One host figured as long as it was liquid it was mixable; another knew what went with what.

Those unwept days are behind us. There is no excuse any more—at restaurant, bar or home—for using anything but the best ingredients or mixing anything but the best drinks. This book contains, I like to think, *all* the better known and most popular drinks as well as a civilized selection of odd-balls, not so often encountered. Some you wouldn't serve to your tax collector; some, just because they're novel, doesn't make them bad. You might very well be the first on your block to offer a Blue Monday or a Smiler—and you might just be starting a vogue.

Another thing worth discussion—the occasion. Just as you wouldn't want steak *every* night, no matter how much you liked steak, so your favorite drink is deserving of a variant now and then, and the time and event might be the determinant. Let me be explicit. A drink or two before a fine dinner, at which a decent wine is to be served, is not exactly the same "occasion" as a cocktail party to celebrate Camp Meddibemps win over Camp Kare Free at archery. The first event suggests abstemiousness on the part of the guests—a drink or even two but certainly no more. At my house, that's the imperative, and late arrivals don't even get two. Else, why bother to prepare a good meal? For the cocktail party, let common sense be your (and their) guide. This I will say—too much or too many of anything is no good. The olives in the Martinis and the cherries in the Manhattans are very indigestible!

It might just interest you to know what your kinsmen are drinking these days—or were, a very little while ago when the survey was made. The Bar-Server Handbook listed the first thirty-two drinks in order of popularity as follows:

		Percent of Mentions
1.	Martini	13.6%
2.	Manhattan	8.5
3.	Vodka Martini	8.1
4.	Scotch/Water	7.0
5.	Bloody Mary	5.1
6.	Scotch	4.4
7.	Whiskey Sour	4.0
8.	Vodka	2.9
9.	Vodka/Tonic	2.9
10.	Canadian	2.6
11.	Daiquiri	2.2
12.	Scotch Highball	1.8
13.	Gin/Tonic	1.8
14.	Margarita	1.8
15.	Vodka Gimlet	1.8
16.	Scotch/Soda	1.5
17.	Gimlet	1.5
18.	Whiskey/Water	1.5
19.	Bourbon	1.5
20.	Blended Whiskey	1.5
21.	Bourbon Highball	1.1
22.	Bourbon/Water	1.1
23.	Screwdriver	1.1
24.	Irish Coffee	1.1
25.	Old Fashioned	1.1

26. Canadian/Water	1.1
27. Vodka Sour	.7
28. Scotch Sour	.7
29. Bacardi Cocktail	.7
30. Rum	.7
31. Harvey Wallbanger	.7
32. Highball	.7
Others	13.2

The "Fastest Growing Drinks" looks like this:

	Percent of Mentions
Vodka Drinks	18.6
Harvey Wallbanger	11.9
Wine	8.5
Vodka Martini	6.8
Margarita	6.8
Martini	5.1
Bloody Mary	5.1
Frozen Peppermint Schnapps	3.4
Brandy	3.4
Scotch	3.4
Others	27.1

The only addition to this report I would want to make is to point out the sudden interest in Tequila and its derivatives, which is such a recent development—it is not reflected in the above.

ROBERT J. MISCH

GLOSSARY

Abricotine: One of the many French apricot liqueurs.

Advocaat: An egg, brandy, sugar combination, not unlike eggnog.

Alcools Blancs or **White Alcohols:** The colorless distillates of fruits, berries and roots made in Alsace, Lorraine, Switzerland and the Black Forest. Kirsch (Cherry) is the best known. Others are Framboise (raspberry), Fraise (strawberry), Mirabelle (yellow plum), Prunelle (purple plum), Williams Poire (pear), etc. There are said to be seventeen of them.

Ale: A malt brew (see BEER) darker and bitterer than beer. Alcoholic content about 6 per cent.

Amaretto: An almond-flavored liqueur from Italy.

Amer Picon: A French bitters, with quinine and orange overtones—favorite of the Foreign Legion.

Angostura Bitters: See BITTERS.

Anisette: A colorless liqueur with an anise flavor.

Apéritif: A drink of moderate alcoholic content, taken before meals, ostensibly to give one an appetite.

Applejack: The common name for apple brandy. Sometimes applies to the homemade product.

Aquavit (Akvavit): The national drink of the Scandinavians; caraway is basic though some other flavorings are sometimes used (Finland calls its Aquavit by the name of Finnish Vodka).

Arrack: An oriental drink of high alcoholic content, generally made from rice. Called the original spirit.

Bacardi: A brand of Puerto Rican rum.

Beer: A liquor, generally light-colored, fermented from cereals and malt, flavored with hops. Alcoholic strength about 6 per cent.

Benedictine: One of the oldest of the herb-flavored liqueurs. A Benedictine monk created the recipe which has remained a secret.

Berger: A pastis of Marseilles (licorice-flavored apéritif).

Bitters: An infusion of aromatics, with bitterness as a common denominator: Campari from Italy is an apéritif, as is Pernod and the pastis. The stronger bitters are used by the drop for flavoring: Angostura, Peychaud's, Herbsaint, Abbott's; also, Holland's Boonekamp and Hungarian Unicum. Fernet Branca is primarily used as a stomachic with after-dinner coffee, or as a pick-me-up.

Bottled in Bond: A term meaning that the distiller agreed under law to store his Whiskey in bonded warehouses without paying the excise tax until he was ready to withdraw the Whiskey from the warehouses. The law provides that Whiskey so bottled and stored must be at least four years old and 100 proof. The stamp "Bottled in Bond" is not a guarantee of quality.

Bourbon: A Whiskey distilled from mash not less than 51 per cent of which was corn grain. Must be aged in new barrels. May be a "Blend" when mixed with neutral spirits or a "Blend of Straights" when blended with a number of Bourbons. Sour mash means that some of the previous day's "slop" or left-overs is used as today's "starter."

Brandy: A spirit made from the distillation of wine or fermented fruit mash. Used alone, it refers to the distillate from grape wine only.

Cognac—the special brandy distilled from the wine made from grapes grown in the Charente, around the cities of Cognac and Jarnac, north of Bordeaux.

Armagnac—the special brandy distilled in the Gers province, around the city of Condom in southern France.

Byrrh: A reddish French apéritif wine, flavored with aromatics.

Calisay: A Spanish liqueur with a bitterish aftertaste.

Calvados: A French apple brandy distilled in Normandy.

Campari: Immensely popular Italian bitters, usually served with soda.

Canadian: A generic name for Whiskies produced in Canadian distilleries. Made primarily from corn. New cooperage not required.

Chartreuse: This liqueur comes in two colors and two strengths. Yellow Chartreuse is lighter and the green is heavier. Both are made from a wide variety of herbs and aromatics and were originated by a French order of monks.

Cin: An apéritif by the makers of Cinzano.

Cognac: See BRANDY.

Cointreau: A brand of Triple Sec or orange liqueur. There is a version colored blue.

Cordial Médoc: A brandy-based liqueur from Bordeaux.

Crème de Bananes: A banana-flavored liqueur.

Crème de Cacao: A dark brown liqueur made of cocoa beans, spices and vanilla with a brandy base.

Crème de Cassis: A dark red liqueur, or syrup, made from black currants. The basis of making a "Kir."

Crème de Menthe: A peppermint-flavored liqueur which comes in three colors: white, green or red.

Crème de Rose: A liqueur flavored with rose petals.

Crème de Vanille: A liqueur flavored with vanilla.

Crème de Violette: A lavender-colored liqueur, made from vanilla and cacao with a violet bouquet.

Crème d'Yvette: A liqueur similar to Crème de Violette but with a pronounced violet taste.

Curaçao: A liqueur made from the peel of Curaçao oranges which are grown on the West Indian Island of Curaçao.

Cynar: An Italian apéritif made from artichokes.

Drambouie: A liqueur made from Scotch Whisky and honey.

Dubonnet: A French apéritif wine made from aromatics. It has a slight quinine taste.

Falerum: A West Indian sweetener for Rum drinks.

Fernet Branca: See BITTERS.

Fraise: A brandy made from strawberries.

Framboise: A brandy made from raspberries.

Galliano: An Italian liqueur.

Gin: A liquor made with a neutral spirit base and flavored, generally, with juniper berries. Old Tom Gin is a sweet gin. Holland Gin, because of its heavy body and distinctive flavor, is usually drunk straight. Most American and British Gins are similar, save for individual brand flavorings.

Goldwasser: Orange-based liqueur with flecks of gold leaf (usually Danziger Goldwasser, from that city).

Grain Whiskies: Made from a mash of cereals and corn, distilled at high proof, used as blenders with malt Whiskies to make Scotch. Not unlike U.S. neutral spirits but usually aged.

Grand Marnier: An orange-flavored liqueur used widely in cookery.

Grenadine: A red, artificially flavored syrup for sweetening.

Irish Mist: A liqueur made from Irish Whiskey.

Irish Whiskey: Oldest Whiskey in the world. All malt Whiskies, blended.

Izarra: Liqueurs from the Basque country, yellow and green, following the Chartreuse pattern.

Kahlua: A coffee-flavored liqueur from Mexico.

Kir: Named for the long-time mayor of Dijon. A drink of dry white wine with a splash of Crème de Cassis.

Kirsch: A colorless brandy distilled from a small black cherry.

Kümmel: A colorless liqueur with a caraway flavor.

Light Whiskey: A recent addition to the lexicon of American Whiskeys. Distilled at a relatively high proof and usually blended with aged neutral spirits. Need not be aged in new cooperage, as with Bourbon.

Liqueurs: These alcoholic drinks are usually made by adding an infusion of fruits or herbs to grain alcohol, brandy, Cognac or Whiskey. They are generally served after meals because of their sweetness, but also are frequently used as flavoring in cocktails or punches.

Lochan Ora: A liqueur made by Chivas, from Scotch Whisky.

Malt: Name given to sprouted barley, as used in making Scotch and Irish Whiskies. Malt Whiskies give Scotch and Irish their distinctive flavors. In Scotland, the four malt Whiskies used in blending are Lowland malts, Highland malts, Islays and Campbeltowns, in ascending order of flavor.

Single Malt refers to special Scotch Whiskies which are unblended and bottled as one individual malt Whiskey.

Mandarine: An orange-flavored liqueur.

Maraschino: A strong sweet liqueur with a pronounced bittersweet cherry taste.

Marc: A strong spirit distilled from the pomace, or left-over skins, pits and stems of wine making. Requires long aging. In Italy, called Grappa. Marc de Bourgogne and Marc de Champagne are the best known.

Noyau: A liqueur made with a brandy base flavored with a variety of fruits and bitter almond.

Ojen, Ouzo: Anisettes from, respectively, Spain and Greece.

Orange Bitters: A flavoring with a bittersweet orange taste used in cocktails and other drinks.

Orgeat: A flavoring syrup with a bittersweet almond taste.

Parfait Amour: A purple, almond-y liqueur. Sweet.

Pernod: The present-day substitute for absinthe, which has been banned because of the wormwood used in its manufacture. Pernod is used as an apéritif and as an ingredient in many cocktails.

Proof: The measurement of alcoholic strength. The alcoholic content of the spirit is one half the indicated proof; thus, 100 proof indicates 50 per cent alcohol (the English use a somewhat different system. English 70 proof=U.S. 80 proof, approximately). The alcohol in wine is "by volume" so 12 per cent means 12 per cent and not half as much as proof in spirits.

Prunelle: A liqueur with the fragrance and flavor of plum.

Quinquina: A reddish brown aromatic wine, flavored with quinine and herbs. The word is often used in referring to other apéritif wines.

Raki (also Arrack, Arak): A rough spirit distilled variously in different countries: from grain in Greece; dates in the Middle East; palm sap and/or rice in the East Indies; sugar cane in Java.

Ricard: Another pastis from Marseilles.

Rum: A liquor made from the fermentation and distillation of sugar cane. The color of Rum has nothing to do with its alcoholic content but the flavor of the darker Rums is stronger than that of the light varieties, the result of additional flavoring matter and caramel.

Rye: A Whiskey distilled from mash not less than fifty-one per cent of which was rye grain.

Sabra: An Israeli liqueur, orange with a taste of chocolate.

St. Raphael: Popular French boulevard apéritif.

Sake: A Japanese fermented liquor of 12 per cent to 16 per cent alcohol. Made from fermented rice. Colorless and sweetish, now often used as a mixer.

Sambuca: An Italian sweet liqueur.

Sangria: A wine punch composed of red wine and fruit juices primarily orange. Sometimes brandy is added.

Scotch Whisky: A product of Scotland distilled from a mash of grain, primarily barley.

Slivovitz: A potent plum brandy from Yugoslavia and other Balkan countries.

Sloe Gin: A liqueur made of Gin and sloe berries.

Southern Comfort: An American liqueur with a Bourbon base and a peach flavor.

Strega: An Italian liqueur.

Suze: A bitter French apéritif, from gentian.

Swedish Punch: A pale yellowish liqueur with a slight rum flavor.

Tequila: A Mexican alcoholic drink distilled from pulque.

Tia Maria: A coffee-flavored liqueur from Jamaica.

Tiddy: A liqueur made from Canadian Whiskey.

Triple Sec: A colorless liqueur with a sweet, orange flavor.

Van der Hum: South African liqueur.

Vieille Cure: A secret formula liqueur from near Bordeaux.

Vermouth, Dry: A dry, aromatic apéritif wine, most frequently used in this country as an ingredient for cocktails.

Vermouth, Sweet: An aromatic apéritif wine, sweet and more highly flavored than the dry. Used mainly in cocktails.

Vodka: A drink, formerly from Russia, Poland, and the Baltic states, but now one of the fastest growing white spirits in the U.S.A. The American version is as colorless, odorless and tasteless as it can be made. Imported Russian and Polish Vodkas are flavored.

Whiskey: The general name for liquors of not less than 80 proof distilled from a mash of grain. Only Scotch Whisky is spelled without the *e*.

STANDARD BAR MEASUREMENTS

A. STANDARD BAR MEASUREMENTS

Imperial (Imperiale)—approximately 8 bottles or 6 liters
Gallon—4 quarts or 128 ounces, U.S.
        British Imperial gallon is approximately 1.2
        U.S. gallons or 4½ liters.
Quart—32 ounces (English quart is 40 British fluid ounces).

1 quart	32 ounces
1 pint	16 ounces
⅘ quart (fifth)	25.6 ounces
1 wineglass (average)	4 ounces
1 jigger	1½ ounces
1 pony	1 ounce
1 teaspoon	⅛ ounce (approx.)
2 teaspoons	1 dessertspoon
3 teaspoons	1 tablespoon
1 cup	8 ounces
1 dash	$\frac{1}{32}$ ounce (approx.)
½ bottle wine	12 ounces
1 bottle wine (average)	24 ounces
split of Champagne	6½ ounces
quart of Champagne	26 ounces
Magnum (two bottles)	52 ounces
Jeroboam (four bottles)	104 ounces
Rehoboam (six bottles)	156 ounces
	(1 gallon, 1 pint, 12 ounces)

B. These are some homely expressions, often used, and meaning different things to different people:
    Splash—a generous spoonful.
    Dollop—a good-sized splash.
    Touch—just a few drops.
    3 Fingers—about 3 ounces; *2 fingers*—about 2 ounces.

PUNCH CUP

LARGE BRANDY SNIFTER

HIGHBALL GLASS

PILSNER GLASS

SMALL BRANDY SNIFTER

DELMONICO

BEER MUG

OLD FASHIONED GLASS

WHISKEY SOUR

**LARGE BOWL
WINE GLASS**

CHAMPAGNE GLASS

LIQUEUR GLASS

RHINE WINE GLASS

COCKTAIL GLASS

POUSSE-CAFÉ GLASS

TOM and JERRY MUG

SHERRY GLASS

SHOT GLASS

SILVER or JULEP MUG

CHAMPAGNE

Because of the nature of this very special wine, all drinks using it as a base, regardless of their type, have been placed together in this section.

Alfonso Cocktail
½ Jigger Dubonnet
1 Cube Ice
1 Dash Bitters
1 Lump Sugar
Place the Sugar in a large saucer Champagne glass and sprinkle with Bitters. Add Ice and Dubonnet and fill with iced Champagne. Serve with twist of Lemon Peel.

Barbotage of Champagne
Fill a tumbler ½ full of finely cracked ice. Add 1 dash of Angostura Bitters, 1 teaspoon each of Sugar Syrup and Lemon Juice, and fill with iced Champagne. Stir lightly and serve with twist of Orange Peel.

Blue Train Cocktail
Shake well together with cracked ice, ¼ Brandy and ¼ lightly sweetened Pineapple Juice. Fill glass ½ full with this mixture and fill with iced Champagne.

Champagne Cobbler
Fill a large goblet ⅔ full of cracked ice. Add ½ teaspoon Lemon Juice and ½ teaspoon Curaçao. Stir and add 1 thin slice of Orange and 1 small Pineapple stick. Fill with iced Champagne. Stir lightly again and serve with a straw.

Champagne Cocktail No. 1

Place 1 small lump Sugar in a Champagne glass and sprinkle with 1 small dash Angostura Bitters. Add 1 small twist each Orange and Lemon Peel. Fill with iced Champagne. Muddle gently.

Champagne Cocktail No. 2

Place ⅔ jigger Southern Comfort, 1 dash Angostura Bitters and 1 twist of Lemon Peel in a large saucer Champagne glass. Fill with iced Champagne.

Champagne Cooler

Place in a tall glass, ½ filled with ice, ⅔ jigger Brandy, ⅔ jigger Cointreau and fill up with chilled Champagne. Stir and garnish with Mint.

Champagne Cup No. 1
(for 12 to 16)

Place in a punch bowl, with a block of ice, ½ Pineapple cut in slices, 6 good slivers of Cucumber Rind, 1 box of fresh Strawberries, 3 jiggers Curaçao, 1 quart Soda Water, and stir lightly. Add 2 bottles iced Champagne. Stir lightly again and serve.

Champagne Cup No. 2
(for 10 or 12)

Place in a punch bowl, with a block of ice, 2 tablespoons Powdered Sugar, 2 jiggers Cognac, ½ jigger Curaçao, ¼ jigger Maraschino, ¼ jigger Grand Marnier and 1 Orange, sliced thin and seeded. Add 1 or 2 quarts iced Champagne and decorate with Pineapple, Maraschino Cherries and fresh Mint.

Champagne Fizz

Place the juice of 1 Orange in a highball glass with several ice cubes. Fill with iced Champagne.

Champagne Julep

Crush 4 sprigs Mint with 1 lump of Sugar and a few drops of water in bottom of your tallest highball glass. Half fill with cracked ice and add 1 jigger Brandy. Fill with Champagne and decorate with extra Mint. Serve with straws.

Champagne Punch No. 1
(1 gallon)

Combine in punch bowl ½ pound Powdered Sugar, 1 quart Soda Water, 2 jiggers Brandy, 2 jiggers Maraschino, 2 jiggers Curaçao, 3 jiggers Lemon Juice. Stir together and add block of ice. Pour in 2 or 3 bottles Champagne. Decorate as desired.

Champagne Punch No. 2
(for 18)

Combine in the order named in a large punch bowl, with a block ice, juice of 2 Oranges, juice of 2 Lemons, ½ cup Sugar, ½ cup Light Rum, ½ cup Dark Rum, 1 cup Pineapple Juice. Stir lightly and pour in 2 bottles iced Champagne. Serve in punch glasses, decorated with fruit as desired.

Champagne Punch No. 3 (for 20)
Place 1 quart either Lemon or Orange Ice in a punch bowl. Pour over it 2–3 bottles iced Champagne.

Champagne Punch No. 4 (for 15)
Place large block of ice in punch bowl. Add 2 jiggers Brandy, 2 jiggers Cointreau and 2 bottles iced Champagne.

Champagne Punch No. 5 (for 10)
Combine in punch bowl, with lots of ice, 1 jigger Maraschino, 1 jigger Yellow Chartreuse, 2 jiggers Brandy, 1 pint Soda Water, 2 teaspoons Sugar and 1 bottle iced Champagne.

Champagne Punch No. 6 (for 12)
Combine in punch bowl 1 jigger Brandy, 1 jigger Curaçao, 1 jigger Maraschino, 2 sliced seeded Lemons, 2 sliced seeded Oranges and ½ basket Strawberries or Raspberries. Add 1 bottle iced Soda Water and 2 bottles iced Champagne, or omit the Soda Water and add 3 bottles iced Champagne. Place the punch bowl to chill in a bed of shaved ice and serve.

Champagne Punch No. 7 (Dragoon Punch) (for 20)
This Punch is reputedly the cavalry man's answer to ARTILLERY PUNCH (see Index). Blend in a large punch bowl 3 pints Porter, 3 pints Ale, ½ pint Brandy, ½ pint Sherry, ½ pint Sugar Syrup and 3 Lemons, sliced thin. Immediately before serving, add a block of ice and 2 bottles iced Champagne.

Champagne Punch No. 8 (individual)
Fill a large tumbler or highball glass ½ full of ice. Add the juice of ½ Lemon, ½ jigger Framboise, 1 slice of Orange and fill with iced Champagne. Stir lightly and serve with straws.

Champagne Velvet (Black Velvet)
Half fill a tall glass with iced Stout. Fill with iced Champagne as desired. Pour very slowly or glass will overflow.

French "75"
1 Jigger Dry Gin
⅓ Jigger Lemon Juice
1 Teaspoon Powdered Sugar
Pour into tall glass ½ full of cracked ice, and fill with chilled Champagne.

French "95"
Prepare same as FRENCH "75," using Bourbon Whiskey instead of Gin.

French "125"
Prepare same as FRENCH "75," using Brandy for Gin.

I. B. F. Pick-Me-Up Cocktail
1 Jigger Brandy
3 Dashes Curaçao
3 Dashes Fernet Branca
1 Cube Ice
Place in large saucer Champagne glass and fill with iced Champagne. Squeeze Lemon Peel over top.

King's Peg
Place a piece of ice in a large wine glass. Pour in 1 jigger Brandy and fill with iced Champagne.

London Special
Place in a large highball glass 1 lump Sugar, a large twist Orange Peel, 1 cube of ice, and 2 dashes Peychaud's Bitters. Muddle well and fill with iced Champagne.

Mimosa
Place a cube of ice in large wine glass. Add the juice of ½ Orange. Fill with iced Champagne and stir.

Peach Bowl No. 1
Place in a large goblet 1 washed unpeeled perfect Peach. Cover with iced Champagne. Prick the Peach several times to release the flavor and serve. The Peach, incidentally, is delicious eating after the drink is finished.

Peach Bowl No. 2
This is prepared same as PEACH BOWL No. 1, but with a Brandied Peach and a little of the Syrup. And you don't need to prick the Peach to get the flavor!

Prince of Wales
Place in a shaker 1 dash Angostura Bitters, 1 teaspoon Curaçao, and ½ jigger each Madeira and Brandy. Shake well with ice and strain into a large wine glass. Fill with iced Champagne and serve with a thin slice of Orange.

Queen's Peg
Place a cube of ice in a large wine glass. Add ½ jigger Dry Gin and fill with iced Champagne.

Shandy Gaff (see Champagne Velvet)

Soyer-au-Champagne Cocktail
Place in a large saucer Champagne glass 1 large teaspoon Vanilla Ice Cream, 2 dashes Maraschino, 2 dashes Curaçao, 2 dashes Brandy and stir together gently. Fill with iced Champagne and decorate with a slice of Orange and a Cherry.

COBBLERS

BASIC COBBLER

The Cobbler, which like the Julep is a drink of American origin, is generally served in a large goblet. Fill 2/3 full of shaved or finely cracked ice. Sprinkle with 1 teaspoon fine granulated Sugar, if desired, and pour in 1 or 2 jiggers Claret, Port, Rhine Wine, Sauterne or Sherry; or, if preferred, 1 or 2 jiggers Applejack, Brandy, Gin, Rum, Whiskey or Vodka. Whatever is used the glass should be decorated with a slice of Orange and a small Pineapple stick. Frequently Mint is used.

SPECIAL COBBLERS

Brandy Cobbler
Fill a tumbler 3/4 full of cracked ice. Add 1 teaspoon Curaçao, 1/2 teaspoon Sugar, 1 or 2 jiggers Brandy. Decorate with fruit and serve.

Champagne Cobbler (see Champagne)

Claret Cobbler
Fill a tumbler 1/2 full of cracked ice. Add 1 dash Maraschino, 1 teaspoon each Sugar and Lemon Juice. Fill with Claret and stir. Decorate with fruit and serve.

Port Cobbler
Fill a tumbler 2/3 full of cracked ice. Add 1 teaspoon each Orange Juice and Curaçao. Fill with Port Wine. Decorate with fruit and serve. A very little Sugar may be added if desired.

Rhine Wine Cobbler
Fill a tumbler 1/2 full of cracked ice. Add 1 teaspoon each Sugar and Lemon Juice. Stir lightly and fill with Rhine Wine. Decorate with twist of Lemon Peel and Mint.

Sauterne Cobbler
Prepare same as RHINE WINE COBBLER, omitting Sugar and Mint.

Sherry Cobbler
Fill a tumbler 2/3 full of cracked ice. Add a teaspoon each Sugar and Orange Juice. Fill with Sherry, stir slightly, decorate with fruit and serve.

COCKTAILS—APÉRITIF AND WINE BASES

AMER PICON

Picon
½ Amer Picon
½ Dry Vermouth
Stir well with ice and strain into glass.

Picon Grenadine
1 Jigger Amer Picon
½ Jigger Grenadine
Place with ice cubes in Old-Fashioned glass and fill with Soda Water.

Queer Kir
Chilled Red Wine
Dollop of Amer Picon
Stir well and pour into glass.

AQUAVIT

Danish Clam
In bottom of mixing glass shake a little Salt, Pepper and Cayenne; ½ teaspoon Worcestershire; 1 teaspoon Lemon Juice; 2 Jiggers Aquavit; 1 Jigger Clam Juice; 1 Jigger Tomato Juice. Chill and serve.

BYRRH

Byrrh
⅓ Byrrh
⅓ Rye Whiskey
⅓ Dry Vermouth
Stir well with ice and strain into glass.

Byrrh Cassis
⅔ Byrrh
⅓ Crème de Cassis
Place in glass with ice cubes and fill with Soda Water.

Byrrh Special
½ Byrrh
½ Old Tom Gin
Stir well with ice and strain into glass.

CALISAY

Calisay
½ Calisay
½ Sweet Vermouth
3 Dashes Sugar Syrup
Stir well with ice and strain into glass.

Montauk Riding Club
1 Jigger Calisay
1 Jigger Brandy
3 Dashes Lime Juice
2 Dashes Sugar Syrup
Shake well with ice and strain into glass.

DUBONNET

Appetizer No. 1
1 Jigger Dubonnet
Juice of ½ Orange
Shake well with ice and strain into glass.

Bob Danby
1 Jigger Dubonnet
½ Jigger Brandy
Stir well with ice and strain into glass.

Dubonnet Manhattan
½ Dubonnet
½ Whiskey
Stir well with ice and serve with Cherry.

Mary Garden
½ Dubonnet
½ Dry Vermouth
Stir well with ice and strain into glass. When served with a twist of Lemon Peel, this is called a MERRY WIDOW.

On-the-Rocks
Place twist of Lemon Peel and ice in Old-Fashioned glass. Then fill with Dubonnet.

Sanctuary
½ Dubonnet
¼ Amer Picon
¼ Cointreau
Stir well with ice and strain into glass.

Upstairs
2 Jiggers Dubonnet
Juice of ¼ Lemon
Pour into large cocktail glass with ice cubes and fill with Soda Water.

Weep No More
⅓ Dubonnet
⅓ Brandy
⅓ Lime Juice
1 Dash Maraschino
Stir well with ice and strain into glass.

FERNET BRANCA

Yodel
½ Fernet Branca
½ Orange Juice
Place ice cube in glass and
combine ingredients. Fill with
Soda Water.

LILLET

Burnt Orange
Slice off bits of Orange Rind
about 1″ long. Pour out a glass
of chilled Lillet. Take a bit of
Rind in left hand. Light a match
with right. Quickly bend Rind
outward and touch match to it.
It will "pf-ff-f" as the exuded
orange oil ignites. Plunge Rind
at once into Lillet. Takes a little
practice. Stir and serve.

Roy Howard
½ Lillet
¼ Brandy
¼ Orange Juice
2 Dashes Grenadine
Shake well with ice and strain
into glass.

PERNOD

All drinks that call for Absinthe
may be made with Pernod.

Brunelle
¼ Pernod
¾ Lemon Juice
1½ Teaspoons Sugar
Shake well with ice and strain
into glass.

Button Hook
¼ Pernod
¼ Apricot Brandy
¼ Brandy
¼ White Crème de Menthe
Shake well with ice and strain
into glass.

Duchess
⅓ Pernod
⅓ Dry Vermouth
⅓ Sweet Vermouth
Shake well with ice and strain
into glass.

Frappé (with Pernod)
1 Jigger Pernod
⅓ Jigger Anisette
2 Dashes Angostura Bitters
Shake well with shaved ice and
strain into glass.

Glad Eye
⅔ Pernod
⅓ Peppermint
Shake well with ice and strain
into glass.

Macaroni
⅓ Pernod
⅓ Sweet Vermouth
Shake well with ice and strain
into glass.

Nine-Pick
⅓ Pernod
⅓ Curaçao
⅓ Brandy
1 Egg Yolk
Shake well with ice and strain
into glass.

Nineteen-Pick-Me-Up
⅔ Pernod
⅓ Gin
1 Dash Angostura Bitters
1 Dash Orange Bitters
1 Dash Sugar Syrup
Shake well with ice and strain into glass. Add dash of Soda Water.

Pansy
1 Jigger Pernod
6 Dashes Grenadine
2 Dashes Angostura Bitters
Shake well with ice and strain into glass.

Pernod No. 1
¾ Pernod
¼ Water
1 Dash Sugar Syrup
1 Dash Angostura Bitters
Shake well with ice and strain into glass.

Pernod No. 2
Prepare same as No. 1, using Pernod and Water half and half.

Suisse
1 Jigger Pernod
4 Dashes Anisette
1 Egg White
Shake well with ice and strain into glass. Sugar Syrup may be used in place of Anisette.

Victory
½ Pernod
½ Grenadine
Shake well with ice and strain into glass. Fill with Soda Water.

PORT

Broken Spur
⅔ White Port
⅙ Dry Gin
⅙ Sweet Vermouth
1 Egg Yolk
1 Teaspoon Anisette
Shake well with ice and strain into glass.

Chocolate No. 1
¾ Port
¼ Yellow Chartreuse
1 Egg Yolk
1 Teaspoon Crushed Chocolate
Shake well with ice and strain into glass.

Coffee (See Coffee No. 2 under "Cocktails—Brandy Base")

Devil's
½ Port
½ Dry Vermouth
2 Dashes Lemon Juice
Stir well with ice and strain into glass.

Port No. 1
2 Jiggers Port
1 Dash Brandy
Stir well with ice and strain into glass. Squeeze Orange Peel over top.

Port No. 2
2 Jiggers Port
2 Dashes Curaçao
1 Dash Orange Bitters
1 Dash Angostura Bitters
Stir well with ice and strain into glass.

Port Sangaree
2 Jiggers Port
1 Jigger Water
½ Teaspoon Powdered Sugar
Stir well with ice and strain into
glass.

PUNCH BASE

After-Dinner Special
1 Jigger Swedish Punch
½ Jigger Cherry Brandy
Juice of ½ Lime
Shake well with ice and strain
into glass.

Bombay No. 1
2 Jiggers East Indian Punch
4 Dashes Lemon Juice
Stir well with ice and strain into
glass.

Doctor
1 Jigger Swedish Punch
Juice of 1 Lime
Stir well with ice and strain into
glass.

East and West
¾ East Indian Punch
¼ Light Rum
1 Dash Lemon Juice
Stir well with ice and strain into
glass.

Grand Slam
½ Swedish Punch
¼ Sweet Vermouth
¼ Dry Vermouth
Stir well with ice and strain into
glass.

Hesitation
¾ Swedish Punch
¼ Rye Whiskey
1 Dash Lemon Juice
Stir well with ice and strain into
glass.

Hundred Per Cent
⅔ Swedish Punch
⅙ Lemon Juice
⅙ Orange Juice
2 Dashes Grenadine
Stir well with ice and strain into
glass.

Margaret Duffy
⅔ Swedish Punch
⅓ Brandy
2 Dashes Bitters
Stir well with ice and strain into
glass.

Waldorf No. 1
½ Swedish Punch
¼ Dry Gin
¼ Lemon or Lime Juice
Stir well with ice and strain into
glass.

SHERRY

Adonis
⅔ Dry Sherry
⅓ Sweet Vermouth
1 Dash Orange Bitters
Stir well with ice and strain into
glass.

Bamboo
½ Sherry
½ Sweet Vermouth
1 Dash Angostura Bitters

Stir well with ice and strain into glass.

Bomb (for 6)
6 Jiggers Sherry
1 Jigger Cointreau
1 Jigger Orange Juice
1 Dash Orange Bitters
2 Dashes Pimento Dram
Shake well with shaved ice and serve with an Olive.

Brazil
½ Sherry
½ Dry Vermouth
1 Dash Pernod
1 Dash Angostura Bitters
Stir well with ice and strain into glass. Squeeze Lemon Peel over top.

Byculla
¼ Sherry
¼ Port
¼ Curaçao
¼ Ginger
Stir well with ice and strain into glass.

Coronation No. 1
½ Sherry
½ Dry Vermouth
1 Dash Maraschino
2 Dashes Orange Bitters
Stir well with ice and strain into glass.

Cupid
2 Jiggers Sherry
1 Egg
1 Teaspoon Powdered Sugar
1 Pinch Cayenne Pepper
Shake well with ice and strain into glass.

Duke of Marlborough
½ Sherry
½ Sweet Vermouth
3 Dashes Raspberry Syrup
Juice of 1 Lime
Shake well with ice and strain into glass.

East Indian
½ Sherry
½ Dry Vermouth
1 Dash Orange Bitters
Stir well with ice and strain into glass.

Greenbriar
⅔ Sherry
⅓ Dry Vermouth
1 Dash Peach Bitters
1 Sprig Fresh Mint
Shake well with ice and strain into glass.

Philomel
⅓ Sherry
⅙ Rum
¼ Quinquina
¼ Orange Juice
1 Pinch Pepper
Shake well with ice and strain into glass.

Pineapple (for 6)
Soak 1 cup crushed Pineapple in 4 jiggers Dry White Wine for 2 hours. Add 2 jiggers fresh Pineapple Juice, the juice of ¼ Lemon and 6 jiggers Sherry. Chill the shaker thoroughly but do not put any ice in the mixture. Stir when cold and strain into glasses. Serve with a small wedge of Pineapple in each.

Plain Sherry
2 Jiggers Sherry
2 Dashes Maraschino
2 Dashes Pernod
Shake well with ice and strain
into glass.

Reform
⅔ Sherry
⅓ Dry Vermouth
1 Dash Orange Bitters
Stir well with ice and strain into
glass. Serve with a Cherry.

Sherry
2 Jiggers Sherry
4 Dashes Dry Vermouth
4 Dashes Orange Bitters
Stir well with ice and strain into
glass.

Sherry and Egg
Carefully break 1 Egg into a
cocktail glass, leaving the yolk
intact. Fill the glass with Sherry.

Sherry Twist No. 1 (for 6)
6 Jiggers Sherry
2 Jiggers Dry Vermouth
2 Jiggers Brandy
1½ Jiggers Cointreau
½ Jigger Lemon Juice
1 Small Piece of Cinnamon
Shake well with ice and strain
into glasses.

Sherry Twist No. 2 (for 6)
5 Jiggers Sherry
4 Jiggers Whiskey
1 Jigger Cointreau
Juice of 1 Orange
Juice of ¼ Lemon
2 Cloves
1 Pinch Cayenne Pepper

Shake well with ice and strain
into glasses.

Ship
½ Sherry
⅛ Whiskey
2 Dashes Rum
2 Dashes Prune Syrup
2 Dashes Orange Bitters
Shake well with ice and strain
into glass. A little Sugar may be
added if desired.

Straight Law
⅔ Dry Sherry
⅓ Dry Gin
Stir well with ice and strain into
glass. A twist of Lemon Peel may
be added.

Tuxedo
2 Jiggers Sherry
½ Jigger Anisette
2 Dashes Maraschino
1 Dash Peychaud's Bitters
Stir well with ice and strain into
glass.

Xeres
2 Jiggers Sherry
1 Dash Peach Bitters
1 Dash Orange Bitters
Stir well with ice and strain into
glass.

VERMOUTH

Addington
½ Sweet Vermouth
½ Dry Vermouth
Stir well with ice and strain into
large cocktail glass. Fill with
Soda Water and serve with twist
of Lemon Peel.

Alice Mine
¼ Dry Vermouth
4 Dashes Sweet Vermouth
½ Grand Marnier
¼ Dry Gin
1 Dash Angostura Bitters
Stir well with ice and strain into glass.

Bonsoni
⅔ Sweet Vermouth
⅓ Fernet Branca
Stir well with ice and strain into glass.

Cherry Mixture
½ Sweet Vermouth
½ Dry Vermouth
1 Dash Maraschino
1 Dash Angostura Bitters
Stir well with ice and strain into glass. Serve with a Cherry.

Chrysanthemum
½ Dry Vermouth
½ Benedictine
3 Dashes Pernod
Stir well with ice and strain into glass. Serve with twist of Orange Peel.

Cinzano
2 Jiggers Sweet Vermouth
2 Dashes Orange Bitters
2 Dashes Angostura Bitters
Stir well with ice and strain into glass. Squeeze Orange Peel over top.

Crystal Bronx
½ Dry Vermouth
½ Sweet Vermouth
Juice of ¼ Orange

Pour into large cocktail glass with ice and fill with Soda Water.

Diplomat
⅔ Dry Vermouth
⅓ Sweet Vermouth
1 Dash Maraschino
Stir well with ice and strain into glass. Add Cherry and squeeze Lemon Peel over top.

Fig Leaf
1 Jigger Sweet Vermouth
⅔ Jigger Light Rum
Juice of ½ Lime
1 Dash Angostura Bitters
Shake well with ice and strain into glass.

Green Room
⅔ Dry Vermouth
⅓ Brandy
2 Dashes Curaçao
Stir well with ice and strain.

Harvard Wine
⅔ Jigger Dry Vermouth
½ Jigger Brandy
1 Dash Orange Bitters
Stir well with ice and strain into large cocktail glass and fill up with Soda Water.

Humpty Dumpty
⅔ Dry Vermouth
⅓ Maraschino
Stir well with ice and strain into glass.

Italian
⅔ Sweet Vermouth
⅓ Fernet Branca
2 Dashes Sugar Syrup
1 Dash Pernod

Stir well with ice and strain into glass.

Nineteen
⅔ Dry Vermouth
⅙ Dry Gin
⅙ Kirsch
1 Dash Pernod
4 Dashes Sugar Syrup
Stir well with ice and strain into glass.

Pantomime
1 Jigger Dry Vermouth
1 Egg White
1 Dash Grenadine
1 Dash Orgeat Syrup
Shake well with ice and strain into glass.

Perfect
1 Jigger Dry Vermouth
1 Jigger Sweet Vermouth
1 Jigger Dry Gin
Stir well with ice and strain into glass. Serve with twist of Lemon Peel.

Perpetual
½ Sweet Vermouth
½ Dry Vermouth
4 Dashes Crème d'Yvette
2 Dashes Crème de Cacao
Stir well with ice and strain into glass.

Plain Vermouth (for 6)
10 Jiggers Dry Vermouth
1 Teaspoon Pernod
1 Teaspoon Maraschino
Stir well with ice and strain into glasses. Serve with a Cherry in each.

Queen Elizabeth Wine
⅔ Jigger Dry Vermouth
⅓ Jigger Benedictine
⅓ Lime or Lemon Juice
Stir well with ice and strain into glass.

Raymond Hitchcocktail
2 Jiggers Sweet Vermouth
1 Slice Pineapple
Juice of ½ Orange
1 Dash Orange Bitters
Stir well with ice and strain into glass.

Soul Kiss No. 1
⅓ Dry Vermouth
⅓ Sweet Vermouth
⅙ Dubonnet
⅙ Orange Juice
Stir well with ice and strain into glass.

Spion Kop
½ Dry Vermouth
½ Dubonnet
Stir well with ice and strain into glass.

Third Rail No. 1
1 Jigger Dry Vermouth
1 Dash Curaçao
1 Dash Mint
Stir well with ice and strain into glass. Serve with twist of Lemon Peel.

Trocadero
½ Dry Vermouth
½ Sweet Vermouth
1 Dash Grenadine
1 Dash Orange Bitters

Stir well with ice and strain into glass. Add Cherry and squeeze Lemon Peel over top.

Tropical
⅓ Dry Vermouth
⅓ Maraschino
⅓ Crème de Cacao
1 Dash Orange Bitters
1 Dash Angostura Bitters
Stir well with ice and strain into glass.

Vermouth Apéritif
Place cracked ice in a cocktail glass. Fill with Sweet Vermouth and serve with twist of Lemon Peel.

Vermouth No. 1
2 Jiggers Vermouth, Dry or Sweet
2 Dashes Angostura Bitters
Stir well with ice and strain into glass.

Vermouth No. 2
1½ Jiggers Sweet Vermouth
½ Teaspoon Curaçao
1 Teaspoon Amer Picon
½ Teaspoon Powdered Sugar
1 Dash Angostura Bitters
Stir well with ice and strain into glass. Serve with twist of Lemon Peel and a Cherry.

Vermouth Cassis
2 Jiggers Dry Vermouth
⅔ Jigger Crème de Cassis
Place in glass with ice cubes and fill with Soda Water.

Vermouth Frappé
1½ Jiggers Sweet Vermouth
1 Dash Angostura Bitters
Stir with shaved ice and strain into glass.

Vermouth Half and Half (see Addington on page 12)

Vermouth-on-the-Rocks
Fill Old-Fashioned glass with ice. Pour in Sweet Vermouth and serve with twist of Lemon Peel.

Washington
⅔ Dry Vermouth
⅓ Brandy
2 Dashes Sugar Syrup
2 Dashes Angostura Bitters
Stir well with ice and strain into glass.

Wyoming Swing
½ Sweet Vermouth
½ Dry Vermouth
1 Teaspoon Powdered Sugar
Juice of ¼ Orange
Shake well with ice and strain into glass.

York Special
¾ Dry Vermouth
¼ Maraschino
4 Dashes Orange Bitters
Stir well with ice and strain into glass.

WINE

Kir
Any dry white table wine, chilled, with a dash of Crème de Cassis.

Cassis is sweet and dark red—a liqueur made from black currants. Use only enough to color wine light pink—the darker, the sweeter drink. (A red, or queer Kir is any dry red table wine with a dash of Amer Picon.)

COCKTAILS—BRANDY
AND COGNAC BASES

Alexander No. 1
⅓ Brandy
⅓ Crème de Cacao
⅓ Cream
Shake well with ice and strain into glass.

American Beauty
⅓ Brandy
⅓ Dry Vermouth
⅓ Orange Juice
1 Dash White Crème de Menthe
1 Dash Grenadine
Shake well with ice and strain into glass. Top carefully with a little Port.

Aunt Jemima
⅓ Brandy
⅓ Crème de Cacao
⅓ Benedictine

Pour ingredients carefully into a liqueur glass so that they are in separate layers. Serve after dinner. Any liqueurs may be "layered" if you remember to use the heaviest bodied first, and so on to the lightest.

B. and B.
½ Brandy
½ Benedictine
Serve in a liqueur glass or iced in a cocktail glass. This is an after-dinner drink.

Baltimore Bracer
½ Brandy
½ Anisette
1 Egg White
Shake well with ice and strain into glass.

Barney Barnato
½ Brandy
½ Dubonnet
1 Dash Angostura Bitters
1 Dash Curaçao
Stir well with ice and strain into
glass.

Betsy Ross
1 Jigger Brandy
1 Jigger Port
2 Dashes Angostura Bitters
1 Dash Curaçao
Stir well with ice and strain into
a large cocktail glass. As an eye-
opener this may be made with
the yolk of 1 Egg and 1 teaspoon
of Sugar. Shake with ice and
strain into glass and serve with a
grating of Nutmeg.

Between-the-Sheets
⅓ Brandy
⅓ Cointreau
⅓ Light Rum
Shake well with ice and strain
into glass.

Big Boy
½ Brandy
¼ Cointreau
¼ Sirop de Citron
Stir well with ice and strain into
glass.

Block and Fall
⅓ Brandy
⅓ Cointreau
⅙ Calvados or Apple Brandy
⅙ Pernod
Shake well with ice and strain
into glass.

Bombay
½ Brandy
¼ Sweet Vermouth
¼ Dry Vermouth
2 Dashes Curaçao
1 Dash Pernod
Stir well with ice and strain into
glass.

Bomber
1 Jigger Brandy
⅓ Jigger Cointreau
⅓ Jigger Anisette
⅔ Jigger Vodka
Shake well with ice.

Bonnie Prince Charles
1 Jigger Brandy or Cognac
½ Jigger Drambuie or Lochan
Ora
Juice ½ Lime
Shake with ice cubes.

Booster
2 Jiggers Brandy
4 Dashes Curaçao
1 Egg White
Shake well with ice and strain
into glass. Serve with a grating of
Nutmeg.

Bosom Caresser
⅔ Brandy
⅓ Curaçao
1 Teaspoon Grenadine
1 Egg Yolk
Shake well with ice and strain
into glass.

Brandy
2 Jiggers Brandy
½ Jigger Curaçao
1 Dash Angostura Bitters

Stir well with ice and strain into glass. Serve with twist of Lemon Peel.

Brandy Blazer
2 Jiggers Brandy
1 Small Twist Orange Peel
1 Twist Lemon Peel
1 Lump Sugar
Place Sugar in bottom of shaker and add other ingredients. Stir with a long spoon; blaze for a few seconds and extinguish. Strain into glass. Serve after dinner.

Brandy Champarelle
1 Jigger Brandy
½ Jigger Curaçao
½ Jigger Yellow Chartreuse
½ Jigger Anisette
Shake well with ice.

Brandy Collins
Made as the TOM COLLINS substituting Brandy for Gin.

Brandy Flip
1 Jigger Brandy
1 Whole Egg
1 Teaspoon Sugar
2 Teaspoons Cream (Optional)
Shake with ice cubes. Dust with Nutmeg.

Brandy Gump
2 Jiggers Brandy
2 Dashes Grenadine
Juice of ½ Lemon
Shake well with ice and strain into glass.

Brandy Old-Fashioned
Place lump of Sugar in bottom of Old-Fashioned glass. Sprinkle with 1 dash of Angostura Bitters. Add twist of Lemon Peel and ice cubes and fill as desired with Brandy. Stir and serve.

Brandy Sour
1½ Jiggers Brandy
Juice of ½ Lemon
1 Teaspoon Sugar
Shake well with ice and strain and serve in a Delmonico glass. Add a Cherry and, if you want, a twist of Lemon Peel.

Brandy Special
2 Jiggers Brandy
2 Dashes Curaçao
2 Dashes Sugar Syrup
2 Dashes Bitters
1 Twist of Lemon Peel
Stir with ice and strain into glass.

Brandy Vermouth
¾ Brandy
¼ Sweet Vermouth
1 Dash Angostura Bitters
Stir well with ice and strain into glass.

Builder-Upper
1 Jigger Brandy or Cognac
⅔ Jigger Benedictine
Juice of 1 Lemon
Shake well with ice cubes in tall glass. Fill with Soda.

Cecil Pick-Me-Up
2 Jiggers Brandy
1 Teaspoon Sugar
1 Egg Yolk

Shake well with ice, strain into large cocktail glass and fill with iced Champagne.

Ceylon
1 Jigger Brandy
½ Jigger Dry Vermouth
⅓ Jigger Triple Sec
½ Jigger Dry Sherry
Juice of ½ Lemon
1 Stick of Cinnamon, Broken
(or One Shake Ground
Cinnamon)
Shake well with ice and strain into glass.

Champs Elysées
1 Jigger Cognac or Brandy
½ Jigger Chartreuse
½ Jigger Lemon Juice
⅓ Tablespoon Powdered Sugar
1 Dash Angostura Bitters
Shake well with ice and strain into glass.

Charles
½ Brandy
½ Sweet Vermouth
1 Dash Angostura or Orange
Bitters
Stir well with ice and strain into glass.

Cherry Blossom
1 Jigger Brandy
1 Jigger Cherry Brandy
⅓ Tablespoon Curaçao
½ Tablespoon Lemon Juice
⅓ Tablespoon Grenadine
Shake thoroughly with shaved ice and strain into glass.

Chicago
1 Jigger Brandy
1 Dash Curaçao
1 Dash Angostura Bitters or
Pernod
Stir well with ice and strain into glass frosted with Sugar. Fill with iced Champagne.

City Slicker
⅔ Brandy
⅓ Curaçao
1 Dash Pernod
Shake well with ice and strain into glass.

Classic
½ Brandy
⅙ Curaçao
⅙ Maraschino
⅙ Lemon Juice
Stir well with ice and strain into glass frosted with Sugar. Squeeze Lemon Peel over top.

Coffee No. 1
⅓ Brandy
⅓ Cointreau
⅓ Cold Black Coffee
Shake well with ice and strain into glass. May be served after dinner.

Coffee No. 2
⅔ Brandy
⅓ Port
2 Dashes Curaçao
2 Dashes Sugar Syrup
1 Egg Yolk
Shake well with ice and strain into small glass. Serve with a

grating of Nutmeg. This cocktail has no Coffee in it but if properly made it should be coffee colored.

Cold Deck
½ Brandy
¼ Sweet Vermouth
¼ White Crème de Menthe
Stir well with ice and strain into glass.

Coronation No. 2
⅔ Brandy
⅓ Curaçao
1 Dash Peach Bitters
1 Dash White Crème de Menthe
Stir well with ice and strain into glass.

Corpse Reviver No. 1
½ Brandy
¼ Calvados or Apple Brandy
¼ Sweet Vermouth
Stir well with ice and strain into glass.

Cuban (Using Brandy in Place of Rum)
⅔ Brandy
⅓ Apricot Brandy
Juice of ½ Lemon
Stir well with ice and strain into glass.

Davis Brandy
⅔ Brandy
⅓ Dry Vermouth
4 Dashes Grenadine
1 Dash Angostura Bitters
Stir well with ice and strain into glass.

Deauville
¼ Brandy
¼ Calvados or Apple Brandy
¼ Cointreau
¼ Lemon Juice
Stir well with ice and strain into glass.

Depth-Charge
1 Jigger Brandy
1 Jigger Calvados or Apple Brandy
½ Teaspoon Grenadine
½ Tablespoon Lemon Juice
Shake gently with ice and strain into glass.

Don't Go Near the Water
½ Brandy
⅙ Curaçao
⅙ Maraschino
⅙ Lemon Juice
Shake well with ice and strain into glass frosted with Sugar. Serve with twist of Lemon Peel.

Double Trouble
⅔ Brandy
⅓ Dry Vermouth
4 Dashes Grenadine
1 Dash Angostura Bitters
Shake well with ice and strain into glass.

Dream
⅔ Brandy
⅓ Curaçao
1 Dash Pernod
Stir well with ice and strain into glass.

East India
¾ Brandy
⅛ Pineapple Juice
⅛ Curaçao
1 Dash Angostura Bitters
Stir well with ice and strain into glass.

Egg Sour
1 Jigger Brandy
1 Jigger Curaçao
Juice of ½ Lemon
1 Egg
1 Teaspoon Sugar
Shake well with ice and strain into Delmonico glass.

Fancy
2 Jiggers Cognac
Dash Angostura Bitters
Frost rim of glass with Lemon and Sugar. Shake ingredients thoroughly with ice. Strain into glass and fill with iced Champagne.

Flying Fortress
1 Jigger Cognac
⅓ Jigger Cointreau
⅓ Jigger Anisette
⅔ Jigger Vodka
Shake well with ice and strain into a large glass.

Frank Sullivan
¼ Brandy
¼ Cointreau
¼ Lillet
¼ Lemon Juice
Shake well with ice and strain into glass.

Froupe
½ Brandy
¼ Sweet Vermouth
1 Teaspoon Benedictine
Stir well with ice and strain into glass.

Gazette
½ Brandy
½ Sweet Vermouth
1 Teaspoon Lemon Juice
1 Teaspoon Sugar Syrup
Stir well with ice and strain into glass.

Grenadier
⅔ Brandy
⅓ Ginger Brandy
1 Dash Jamaica Ginger
1 Teaspoon Powdered Sugar
Stir well with ice and strain into glass.

Harry's Pick-Me-Up
2 Jiggers Cognac
1 Teaspoon Grenadine
Juice of ½ Lemon
Shake well with ice and strain into glass. Fill with iced Champagne.

Harvard
½ Brandy
½ Sweet Vermouth
2 Dashes Angostura Bitters
1 Dash Sugar Syrup
Stir well with ice and strain into glass.

Hoop La
¼ Brandy
¼ Lemon Juice
¼ Cointreau
¼ Lillet

Stir well with ice and strain into glass.

Horse's Neck
Same as WHISKEY HORSE'S NECK substituting Brandy for Whiskey.

Ichbien
¾ Brandy
¼ Curaçao
1 Egg Yolk
Milk as desired
Shake well with ice and strain into glass. Sprinkle with Nutmeg. Excellent for the morning after.

Iris (for 6)
4 Jiggers Brandy
1 Jigger Sweet Vermouth
Juice of 1 Lemon
Shake well with ice and strain into glasses.

Italian Stinger
Same as CRÈME DE MENTHE STINGER substituting Galliano for Menthe.

Janet Howard
2 Jiggers Brandy
1 Dash Angostura Bitters
1 Teaspoon Orgeat Syrup
Place cube of ice in cocktail glass and add ingredients. Stir with a spoon and serve with twist of Lemon Peel.

Lady Be Good
½ Brandy
¼ White Crème de Menthe
¼ Sweet Vermouth
Shake with cracked ice and strain into glass.

Let's Slide
½ Brandy
¼ Port
¼ Blackberry Brandy
Shake well with ice and strain into glass.

Lugger
½ Brandy
½ Calvados or Apple Brandy
1 Dash Apricot Brandy
Stir with ice and strain into glass. Serve with twist of Orange Peel.

Mabel Tea
1 Jigger Brandy
⅓ Jigger Amer Picon
Juice of ½ Lime
Shake well with ice and strain into glass.

Metropolitan
½ Brandy
½ Sweet Vermouth
2 Dashes Sugar Syrup
1 Dash Angostura Bitters
Stir well with ice and strain into glass.

Mikado
1 Jigger Brandy
2 Dashes Curaçao
2 Dashes Orgeat Syrup
2 Dashes Crème de Noyau
2 Dashes Angostura Bitters
Stir well with ice and strain into glass.

Moonraker
⅓ Brandy
⅓ Peach Brandy
⅓ Quinquina
3 Dashes Pernod

Shake well with ice and strain into glass.

Morning
½ Brandy
½ Dry Vermouth
2 Dashes Pernod
2 Dashes Maraschino
2 Dashes Curaçao
2 Dashes Orange Bitters
Stir well with ice and strain into glass. Squeeze Lemon Peel over top and serve with a Cherry.

Mrs. Solomon
1 Jigger Brandy
2 Dashes Curaçao
2 Dashes Angostura or Orange Bitters
Stir with ice and strain into glass frosted with Sugar. Serve with twist of Lemon Peel.

Newton's Special
¾ Brandy
¼ Cointreau
1 Dash Angostura Bitters
Stir well with ice and strain into glass.

Nick's Own
½ Brandy
½ Sweet Vermouth
1 Dash Angostura Bitters
1 Dash Pernod
Stir well with ice and strain into glass. Squeeze Lemon Peel over top and serve with a Cherry.

Nicolaski
Chill 1 or 2 jiggers Brandy with ice. Pour into cocktail glass and add 1 slice Lemon dipped in Powdered Sugar.

Night Cap
⅓ Brandy
⅓ Curaçao
⅓ Anisette
1 Egg Yolk
Shake well with ice and strain into glass.

None but the Brave
⅔ Brandy
⅓ Pimento Dram
1 Teaspoon Powdered Sugar
1 Dash of Jamaica Ginger
1 Dash Lemon Juice
Shake well with ice and strain into glass.

Normandy (for 6)
3 Jiggers Brandy
2 Jiggers Calvados or Apple Brandy
1 Jigger Dry Gin
4 Jiggers Sweet Cider
Shake well with ice and strain into glasses.

Odd McIntyre
¼ Brandy
¼ Cointreau
¼ Lillet
¼ Lemon Juice
Stir well with ice and strain into glass.

Olympic
⅓ Brandy
⅓ Curaçao
⅓ Orange Juice
Stir well with ice and strain into glass.

Peppermint Stick
1 Jigger Brandy
3 Dashes Curaçao
1 Dash Peach Bitters
1 Dash Peppermint
Shake well with ice and strain
into glass.

Peter Tower
⅔ Brandy
⅓ Light Rum
1 Teaspoon Grenadine
1 Teaspoon Curaçao
1 Teaspoon Lemon Juice
Shake well with ice and strain
into glass.

Phoebe Snow
½ Brandy
½ Dubonnet
1 Dash Pernod
Stir well with ice and strain into
glass.

Poop Deck (see Let's Slide)

Pousse Café
(Note: There is no *one* way to do
this. It all depends on specific
gravity as each liquid must float
atop the previous one poured, so
that you get a rainbow of colors.)
¼ Jigger Grenadine
¼ Jigger Maraschino
¼ Jigger Green Crème de Menthe
¼ Jigger Crème de Violette
¼ Jigger Green Chartreuse
¼ Jigger Brandy
Pour ingredients one at a time
into glass, starting with
Grenadine.

or

¼ Jigger Maraschino
¼ Jigger Raspberry Syrup
¼ Jigger Crème de Cacao
¼ Jigger Curaçao
¼ Jigger Yellow Chartreuse
¼ Jigger Brandy
Pour ingredients one at a time
into glass, starting with
Maraschino.

Prairie Oyster No. 1
1 Jigger Brandy
1 Egg
1 Dash Worcestershire Sauce
Salt if desired
Carefully break egg into 6 ounce
glass. Add Worcestershire Sauce
and Brandy. Blend lightly with
Egg White, keeping Yolk intact.
For the morning after.

Presto
⅔ Brandy
⅓ Sweet Vermouth
1 Dash Orange Juice
1 Dash Pernod
Stir well with ice and strain into
glass.

Quaker's
⅓ Brandy
⅓ Rum
⅙ Lemon Juice
⅙ Raspberry Syrup
Shake well with ice and strain
into glass.

Queen Elizabeth
½ Brandy
½ Sweet Vermouth
1 Dash Curaçao
Stir well with ice and strain into
glass. Add a Cherry if desired.

Quelle Vie
⅔ Brandy
⅓ Kümmel
Stir well with ice and strain into glass.

Ray Long
1½ Jiggers Brandy
¾ Jigger Sweet Vermouth
4 Dashes Pernod
1 Dash Angostura Bitters
Stir well with ice and strain into glass.

Rock-a-Bye (same as Froupe)

Saratoga No. 1
2 Jiggers Brandy
2 Dashes Maraschino
2 Dashes Angostura Bitters
¼ Slice Pineapple
Shake well with ice and strain.
Add a little Soda Water if desired.

Saucy Sue
½ Brandy
½ Calvados or Apple Brandy
1 Dash Apricot Brandy
1 Dash Pernod
Stir well with ice and strain into glass. Squeeze Orange Peel over top.

Savoy Hotel
⅓ Brandy
⅓ Benedictine
⅓ Crème de Cacao
Pour ingredients carefully into liqueur glass so that they do not mix. Serve after dinner.

Sidecar
½ Brandy
¼ Cointreau
¼ Lemon Juice
Shake well with ice and strain into glass.

Sink or Swim
¾ Brandy
¼ Sweet Vermouth
1 Dash Angostura Bitters
Stir well with ice and strain into glass.

Sir Ridgeway Knight
⅔ Jigger Brandy
⅔ Jigger Triple Sec
⅔ Jigger Yellow Chartreuse
2 Dashes Angostura Bitters
Shake well with ice and strain into glass.

Sir Walter
⅔ Brandy
⅓ Light Rum
1 Teaspoon Grenadine
1 Teaspoon Curaçao
1 Teaspoon Lemon Juice
Shake well with ice and strain into glass.

Sledge Hammer
⅓ Brandy
⅓ Rum
⅓ Apple Brandy
1 Dash Pernod
Shake well with ice and strain into glass.

Sleepy Head
2 Jiggers Brandy
1 Twist Orange Peel
4 Leaves Fresh Mint, slightly
crushed
1–2 Cubes Ice
Combine in Old-Fashioned glass
and fill with ginger ale.

Southern Cross
1 Jigger Brandy
1 Jigger Medium Rum
Juice of ½ Lime
½ Teaspoon Sugar
Dash Curaçao
Dollop Club Soda
Shake well with ice adding Soda
at end.

Stinger
½ Brandy
½ White Crème de Menthe
Shake well with shaved ice and
strain into glass.

Stomach Reviver
⅓ Brandy
⅓ Kümmel
⅙ Angostura Bitters
⅙ Fernet Branca
Stir well with ice and strain into
glass. For the morning after.

Sweeney's
1 Jigger Brandy
⅓ Jigger Pineapple Juice
1 Dash Maraschino
3 Dashes Angostura Bitters
Shake well with ice and strain
into glass.

Tantalus
⅓ Brandy
⅓ Forbidden Fruit Liqueur
⅓ Lemon Juice
Shake well with ice and strain
into glass.

The Devil
⅔ Jigger Brandy
⅔ Jigger Green Crème de
Menthe
1 Pinch Red Pepper
Shake Brandy and Crème de
Menthe and strain into glass.
Sprinkle Red Pepper on top.

Third Rail No. 2
⅓ Brandy
⅓ Calvados or Apple Brandy
⅓ Light Rum
1 Dash Pernod
Shake well with ice and strain
into glass.

Three Miller
⅔ Brandy
⅓ Light Rum
1 Dash Lemon Juice
1 Teaspoon Grenadine
Stir well with ice and strain.

Thunder or Thunder and Lightning
2 Jiggers Brandy
1 Teaspoon Sugar Syrup
1 Egg Yolk
1 Pinch Cayenne Pepper
Shake well with ice and strain
into glass.

Tin Wedding
¾ Jigger Brandy
¾ Jigger Dry Gin
¾ Jigger Sweet Vermouth
2 Dashes Orange Bitters
Shake well with ice and strain
into glass.

Vanderbilt Hotel
¾ Brandy
¼ Cherry Brandy
2 Dashes Angostura Bitters
2 Dashes Sugar Syrup
Stir well with ice and strain into
glass.

Wallick's Special
1 Jigger Brandy
1 Jigger Cream
1 Egg White
½ Teaspoon Powdered Sugar
2 Dashes Grenadine
Shake well with ice and strain
into glass.

Ward's
½ Jigger Brandy
½ Jigger Chartreuse
1 Twist Orange Peel
Arrange the Orange Peel in
bottom of glass to form a circle.
Fill it with finely cracked ice and
add the Chartreuse and Brandy
and decorate with Fresh Mint
Leaves. Different Liqueurs may
be used if desired.

Waterbury
2 Jiggers Brandy
1 Egg White
Juice of ¼ Lemon
½ Teaspoon Powdered Sugar
2 Dashes Grenadine

Shake well with ice and strain
into glass.

W.C.T.U.
1 Jigger Brandy
1 Jigger Dry Vermouth
Dash Angostura Bitters
Dash Orange Bitters
Shake quickly with shaved ice
and strain into glass. Serve with
a twist of Lemon Peel.

Whip
½ Brandy
¼ Sweet Vermouth
¼ Dry Vermouth
3 Dashes Curaçao
1 Dash Pernod
Shake well with ice and strain
into glass.

White Way
⅓ Brandy
⅓ Anisette
⅓ Pernod
Stir well with ice and strain into
glass.

Why Marry?
⅜ Brandy
⅛ Dry Gin
⅛ Cointreau
⅛ Lemon Juice
Shake well with ice and strain
into glass.

William of Orange
⅔ Brandy
⅓ Curaçao
1 Dash Orange Bitters
Stir well with ice and strain into
glass.

Willie Smith
⅔ Brandy
⅓ Maraschino
1 Dash Lemon Juice
Stir well with ice and strain into
glass.

W. Johnson Quinn
½ Brandy
¼ Sweet Vermouth
¼ Dry Vermouth
3 Dashes Curaçao
1 Dash Grenadine
Stir well with ice and strain into
glass.

Yes and No
2 Jiggers Brandy
4 Dashes Curaçao
1 Egg White

Shake well with ice and strain
into glass. Sprinkle with grating
of Nutmeg.

Young Man
¾ Brandy
¼ Sweet Vermouth
2 Dashes Curaçao
1 Dash Angostura Bitters
Stir well with ice and strain into
glass.

Zoom
1½ Jiggers Brandy
⅓ Jigger Honey
½ Jigger Cream
Shake with ice and strain into
glass.

COCKTAILS—CALVADOS, APPLEJACK OR APPLE BRANDY BASE

A.J.
½ Applejack
½ Unsweetened Grapefruit Juice
Grenadine to taste
Shake well with ice and strain into glass.

Ante
½ Calvados or Apple Brandy
¼ Cointreau
¼ Dubonnet
1 Dash Angostura Bitters
Stir well with ice and strain into glass.

Apple
⅓ Calvados or Apple Brandy
⅙ Brandy
⅙ Gin
⅓ Sweet Cider
Stir well with ice and strain into glass.

Applejack No. 1
1 Jigger Applejack
1 Teaspoon Sugar Syrup
2 Dashes Orange Bitters
1 Dash Angostura Bitters
Stir well with ice and strain into glass.

Applejack No. 2
¾ Calvados or Apple Brandy
¼ Sweet Vermouth
1 Dash Angostura Bitters
Stir well with ice and strain into glass.

Applejack Rabbit
1 Jigger Applejack or Apple Brandy
⅓ Jigger Lemon Juice
⅓ Jigger Orange Juice
Maple Syrup to taste
Shake well with ice and strain into glass.

Applejack Sour
2 Jiggers Applejack
Juice of ½ Lime
Juice of ½ Lemon
1 Dash Grenadine
½ Teaspoon Sugar
Shake well with ice and strain
into Delmonico glass. Decorate
with fruit if desired.

Barton Special
½ Calvados or Apple Brandy
¼ Scotch Whisky
¼ Dry Gin
Shake well with ice and strain
into glass. Serve with twist of
Lemon Peel.

Bentley
½ Calvados or Apple Brandy
½ Dubonnet
Stir well with ice and strain into
glass.

B.V.D.
Prepare same as APPLEJACK No.
2, omitting Bitters. Serve with
twist of Lemon Peel.

Calvados
⅓ Calvados or Apple Brandy
⅓ Orange Juice
⅙ Cointreau
⅙ Orange Bitters
Stir well with ice and strain into
glass.

Castle Dip
½ Apple Brandy
½ White Crème de Menthe
3 Dashes Pernod
Shake well with ice and strain
into glass.

Depth Bomb
1 Jigger Applejack
1 Jigger Brandy
¼ Teaspoon Grenadine
¼ Teaspoon Lemon Juice
Shake well with ice and strain
into glass.

Dick Molnar or Diki-Diki
⅔ Calvados or Apple Brandy
⅙ Swedish Punch
⅙ Grapefruit Juice
Stir well with ice and strain into
glass.

Honeymoon
1 Jigger Applejack
½ Jigger Benedictine
Juice of ½ Lemon
3 Dashes Curaçao
Shake well with ice and strain
into glass.

Jack-in-the-Box
1 Jigger Applejack
½ Jigger Pineapple Juice
Juice of ½ Lemon
2 Dashes Angostura Bitters
Shake well with ice and strain
into glass.

Jack Rose
1 Jigger Applejack
⅓ Jigger Grenadine
Juice of ½ Lime
Shake well with ice and strain
into glass.

Jersey Lightning
2 Jiggers Applejack
1 Dash Angostura Bitters
Sugar Syrup to taste
Shake well with ice and strain
into glass.

Kenny (for 4)
3 Jiggers Applejack
2 Jiggers Sweet Vermouth
Juice of ½ Lemon
1 Dash Angostura Bitters
2 Dashes Grenadine
Shake well with ice and strain
into glasses.

Liberty
⅔ Applejack
⅓ Light Rum
1 Dash Sugar Syrup
Shake well with ice and strain
into glass.

Oom Paul
½ Calvados or Apple Brandy
½ Dubonnet
1 Dash Angostura Bitters
Stir well with ice and strain into
glass.

Philadelphia Scotchman
⅓ Applejack
⅓ Port
⅓ Orange Juice
Place in large cocktail glass with
cracked ice and fill with Soda
Water.

Princess Mary's Pride
½ Calvados or Apple Brandy
¼ Dubonnet
¼ Dry Vermouth
Stir well with ice and strain into
glass.

Roulette
½ Calvados or Apple Brandy
¼ Light Rum
¼ Swedish Punch
Stir well with ice and strain into
glass.

Royal Smile
½ Applejack
¼ Dry Gin
¼ Grenadine
Juice of ¼ Lemon
Shake well with ice and strain
into glass.

Sharky Punch
¾ Calvados or Apple Brandy
¼ Rye Whiskey
1 Teaspoon Sugar Syrup
Shake well with ice and strain
into glass. Add dash of Soda
Water.

Special Rough
½ Applejack
½ Brandy
1 Dash Pernod
Stir with shaved ice and strain
into glass.

Star No. 1
½ Applejack
½ Sweet Vermouth
1 Dash Orange Bitters
Stir with cracked ice and strain
into glass. Sugar Syrup may be
added if desired.

Stone Fence No. 1
2 Jiggers Applejack
1–2 Dashes Angostura Bitters
Place in tall glass with ice and
fill with Cider.

Tinton
⅔ Applejack
⅓ Port Wine
Stir well with ice and strain into
glass.

Torpedo
⅔ Calvados or Apple Brandy
⅓ Brandy
1 Dash Gin
Stir well with ice and strain into
glass.

Tulip
⅓ Calvados or Apple Brandy
⅓ Sweet Vermouth
⅙ Apricot Brandy
⅙ Lemon Juice
Stir well with ice and strain into
glass.

Twelve Miles Out
⅓ Calvados or Apple Brandy
⅓ Light Rum
⅓ Swedish Punch

Stir well with ice and strain into
glass. Squeeze Orange Peel over
top.

Whist
½ Calvados or Apple Brandy
¼ Light Rum
¼ Sweet Vermouth
Stir well with ice and strain into
glass.

Widow's Kiss
½ Calvados or Apple Brandy
¼ Yellow Chartreuse
¼ Benedictine
1 Dash Angostura Bitters
Shake well with ice and strain
into glass.

COCKTAILS—GIN BASE

Abbey
½ Dry Gin
¼ Lillet
¼ Orange Juice
1 Dash Angostura Bitters
Stir well with ice and strain into
glass. Serve with a twist of
Orange Peel or Cherry.

Absinthe
1 Jigger Gin
⅔ Jigger Pernod
Dash Angostura
Dash Grenadine
Shake with cracked ice.

Alaska
¾ Dry Gin
¼ Yellow Chartreuse
2 Dashes Orange Bitters
Stir well with ice and strain into
glass. Serve with a twist of
Lemon Peel.

Alexander No. 2
½ Dry Gin
¼ Crème de Cacao
¼ Cream
Shake well with ice and strain
into glass. (See Index for
ALEXANDER NO. 1 with Brandy
Base.)

Alexander's Sister
½ Dry Gin
¼ Crème de Menthe
¼ Cream
Shake well with ice and strain
into glass.

Alfonso Special
¼ Dry Gin
¼ Dry Vermouth
½ Grand Marnier
4 Dashes Sweet Vermouth
1 Dash Angostura Bitters
Shake well with ice and strain
into glass.

Allen Special
⅔ Dry Gin
⅓ Maraschino
1 Dash Lemon Juice
Stir well with ice and strain into
glass.

Allies
½ Dry Gin
½ Dry Vermouth
2 Dashes Kümmel
Stir well with ice and strain into
glass.

Angel Face
⅓ Dry Gin
⅓ Apricot Brandy
⅓ Calvados or Apple Brandy
Stir well with ice and strain into
glass.

Apparent
½ Dry Gin
½ Dubonnet
1 Dash Pernod
Shake well with ice and strain
into glass.

Appetizer No. 2 or Dubonnet
½ Dry Gin
½ Dubonnet
Stir well with ice and strain into
glass. The juice of ½ Orange
or a dash of Angostura Bitters
may be added if desired.

Artillery
⅔ Dry Gin
⅓ Sweet Vermouth
2 Dashes Bokers or Angostura
Bitters

Stir well with ice and strain into
glass. Serve with a twist of
Lemon Peel.

Astoria
⅔ Dry Gin
⅓ Dry Vermouth
1 Dash Orange Bitters
Stir well with ice and strain into
glass. Serve with an Olive.

Atta Boy
⅔ Dry Gin
⅓ Dry Vermouth
4 Dashes Grenadine
Stir well with ice and strain into
glass. Serve with a twist of
Lemon Peel.

Attention
¼ Dry Gin
¼ Pernod
¼ Dry Vermouth
¼ Crème de Violette
2 Dashes Orange Bitters
Stir well with ice and strain into
glass.

Atty
¾ Dry Gin
¼ Dry Vermouth
3 Dashes Crème de Violette
Stir well with ice and strain into
glass. Serve with a twist of
Lemon Peel. A dash or two of
Pernod also may be added.

Aviation
⅔ Dry Gin
⅓ Lemon Juice
2 Dashes Maraschino
2 Dashes Apricot Brandy

Stir well with ice and strain into glass.

Barbary Coast
¼ Dry Gin
¼ Scotch Whisky
¼ Crème de Cacao
¼ Cream
Shake well with ice and strain into small highball or Old-Fashioned glass.

Barking Dog
⅓ Dry Gin
⅓ Dry Vermouth
⅓ Sweet Vermouth
2 Dashes Calisay
Stir well with ice and strain into glass. Serve with a Cherry.

Barnum
⅔ Dry Gin
⅓ Apricot Brandy
2 Dashes Angostura Bitters
1 Dash Lemon or Lime Juice
Shake well with ice and strain into glass.

Baron
⅔ Dry Gin
⅓ Dry Vermouth
6 Dashes Curaçao
2 Dashes Sweet Vermouth
Stir well with ice and strain into glass. Serve with a twist of Lemon Peel.

Beauty Spot
⅔ Gin
⅓ Grenadine
1 Egg White
Shake well with ice and strain into glass.

Bees' Knees
1 Jigger Gin
1 Teaspoon Honey
Juice of ¼ Lemon
Shake well with ice and strain into glass.

Belmont
⅔ Gin
⅓ Grenadine or Raspberry Syrup
½ Jigger Cream
Shake well with ice and strain into glass.

Bennett
¾ Dry Gin
¼ Lime Juice
1–2 Dashes Angostura Bitters
1 Teaspoon Powdered Sugar (optional)
Shake well with ice and strain into glass.

Bermuda Rose
1 Jigger Dry Gin
1 Dash Grenadine
1 Dash Apricot Brandy
⅓ Jigger Lemon or Lime Juice
Shake well with ice and strain into glass.

Berry Wall
½ Dry Gin
½ Sweet Vermouth
4 Dashes Curaçao
Stir with ice and strain into glass. Twist a Lemon Peel just over the top and serve with a Cherry.

Best Home-Made
1–2 Jiggers Gin
Juice of ½ Orange

Shake well with ice and strain into glass.

Bich's Special
⅔ Dry Gin
⅓ Lillet
1 Dash Angostura Bitters
Stir well with ice and strain into glass. Squeeze Orange Peel over top.

Biffy
½ Dry Gin
¼ Swedish Punch
¼ Lemon Juice
Stir well with ice and strain into glass.

Bijou
⅓ Dry Gin
⅓ Green Chartreuse
⅓ Sweet Vermouth
1 Dash Orange Bitters
Stir well with ice and strain into glass. Serve with a twist of Lemon Peel.

Bill Lyken's Delight
½ Dry Gin
½ Sweet Vermouth
4 Dashes Curaçao
1 Twist Lemon Peel
1 Twist Orange Peel
Stir well with ice and strain into glass.

Bitter
½ Dry Gin
¼ Lemon Juice
¼ Green Chartreuse
1 Dash Pernod
Shake well with ice and strain into glass. A pinch of Sugar may be added if desired.

Blackthorn
½ Sloe Gin
½ Sweet Vermouth
2 Dashes Orange Bitters
Stir well with ice and strain into glass. Twist Lemon Peel over top and serve with a Cherry.

Blenton
⅔ English Gin
⅓ Dry Vermouth
1 Dash Angostura Bitters
Stir well with ice and strain into glass. Twist Lemon Peel over top and serve with a Cherry.

Bloodhound
½ Dry Gin
¼ Dry Vermouth
¼ Sweet Vermouth
2–3 Crushed Strawberries
Stir well with ice and strain into glass.

Bloody Mary
(also made with Vodka)
1 Jigger Gin
2 Jiggers Tomato Juice
⅓ Jigger Lemon Juice
Dash Worcestershire Sauce
Salt and Pepper
Dash Tabasco
Shake well and strain into large glass.

Blue Bird
2 Jiggers Dry Gin
4 Dashes Angostura Bitters
4 Dashes Curaçao
Stir well with ice and strain into glass. Twist Lemon Peel over top and serve with a Cherry.

Blue Devil
½ Dry Gin
¼ Maraschino
¼ Lemon or Lime Juice
1 Dash Blue Vegetable Extract
(coloring)
Shake well with ice and strain
into glass.

Blue Moon
1 Jigger Dry Gin
⅓ Jigger Maraschino
1 Egg White
Shake well with ice and strain
into glass.

Blue Train
½ Dry Gin
¼ Lemon Juice
¼ Cointreau
1 Dash Blue Vegetable Extract
(coloring)
Shake well with ice and strain
into glass.

Bon Appetit
½ Dry Gin
½ Dubonnet
3 Dashes Angostura Bitters
Juice of ½ Orange
Shake well with ice and strain
into glass.

Breakfast
⅔ Dry Gin
⅓ Grenadine
1 Egg White
Shake well with ice and strain
into glass.

Bronx (dry)
¾ Dry Gin
¼ Dry Vermouth
Juice of ¼ Orange
Stir well with ice and strain into
glass.

Bronx (sweet)
½ Dry Gin
¼ Dry Vermouth
¼ Sweet Vermouth
Juice of ¼ Orange
Stir well with ice and strain into
glass.

Bronx Golden
Follow directions for BRONX
(sweet) adding Yolk of 1 Egg.

Bronx River
⅔ Jigger Dry Gin
⅓ Jigger Sweet Vermouth
Juice of 1 Lemon
½ Teaspoon Sugar
Stir well with ice and strain into
glass.

Bronx Silver or Oriental
Follow directions for BRONX
(sweet) adding the White of 1
Egg and 1 slice Pineapple.

Buby
½ Dry Gin
½ Lemon Juice
1 Teaspoon Grenadine
Shake well and strain into glass.

Bulldog
Place 2–3 cubes in a large Old-
Fashioned glass. Add 2 jiggers
Gin, the juice of 1 Orange and
fill with Ginger Ale. Stir slightly
and serve . . . sometimes with a
straw.

Bunny Hug
1/3 Dry Gin
1/3 Whiskey (Bourbon or
Blend)
1/3 Pernod
Shake well with ice and strain
into glass.

B.V.D.
1/3 Dry Gin
1/3 Light Rum
1/3 Dry Vermouth
Stir well with ice and strain into
glass.

Cabaret
1/2 Dry Gin
1/2 Dubonnet
1 Dash Pernod
1 Dash Angostura Bitters
Stir well with ice and strain into
glass. Serve with a Cherry.

Café de Paris
2 Jiggers Dry Gin
3 Dashes Anisette
1 Teaspoon Cream
1 Egg White
Shake well with ice and strain
into glass.

Campden
1/2 Dry Gin
1/4 Cointreau
1/4 Lillet
Stir well with ice and strain into
glass. Serve with a Cherry.

Caruso
1/3 Dry Gin
1/3 Dry Vermouth
1/3 Green Crème de Menthe
Stir well with ice and strain into
glass.

Casino
2 Jiggers Old Tom Gin
2 Dashes Maraschino
2 Dashes Orange Bitters
2 Dashes Lemon Juice
Stir well with ice and strain into
glass.

Cat's Eye
1/3 Jigger Dry Gin
1/6 Jigger Lemonade
1/6 Teaspoon Kirsch
1/3 Jigger Dry Vermouth
1 Dash Cointreau
Shake well with ice and strain
into glass. Serve with a twist of
Lemon Peel.

C.F.H.
1/3 Dry Gin
1/6 Calvados or Apple Brandy
1/6 Swedish Punch
1/6 Grenadine
1/6 Lemon Juice
Shake well with ice and strain
into glass.

Chanticleer
2 Jiggers Dry Gin
Juice of 1/2 Lemon
1 Tablespoon Raspberry Syrup
1 Egg White
Shake well with ice and strain
into glass.

Chappelle
Muddle 2–3 slices of Pineapple
in a shaker. Add:
1/2 Jigger Sweet Vermouth
1/2 Jigger Dry Gin
Juice of 1/2 Lime
Shake well with ice and strain
into glass.

Charleston

⅙ Dry Gin
⅙ Kirsch
⅙ Maraschino
⅙ Curaçao
⅙ Dry Vermouth
⅙ Sweet Vermouth
Stir well with ice and strain into glass. Squeeze Lemon Peel over top.

Charlie Lindbergh

½ English Gin
½ Lillet
2 Dashes Apricot Brandy
2 Dashes Orange Juice
Stir well with ice and strain into glass. Squeeze Lemon Peel over top.

Chatterley

½ Dry Gin
¼ Dry Vermouth
⅛ Orange Juice
⅛ Curaçao
Shake well with ice and strain into glass.

Chorus Lady

⅓ Dry Gin
⅓ Dry Vermouth
⅓ Sweet Vermouth
Juice of ¼ Orange
Stir well with ice and strain into glass. Serve with slice of Orange and a Cherry.

Church Parade

⅔ English Gin
⅓ Dry Vermouth
1 Dash Curaçao
4 Dashes Orange Juice
Stir well with ice and strain into glass. Serve with a Cherry.

Claridge

⅓ Dry Gin
⅓ Dry Vermouth
⅙ Apricot Brandy
⅙ Cointreau
Stir well with ice and strain into glass. Serve with a Cherry.

Clover Club

⅔ Dry Gin
⅓ Grenadine
Juice of ½ Lime
1 Egg White
Shake well with ice and strain into glass.

Clover Leaf

Prepare same as a CLOVER CLUB but serve with a Mint Leaf in each glass.

Club

⅔ Dry Gin
⅓ Sweet Vermouth
Stir well with ice and strain into glass. Serve with a Cherry or an Olive.

Colonial

⅔ Dry Gin
⅓ Grapefruit Juice
3 Dashes Maraschino
Shake well with ice and strain into glass.

Come Again

1 Jigger Dry Gin
2 Dashes Peach Bitters
2 Sprigs Fresh Mint
Shake with shaved ice and strain into glass.

Cooperstown
½ Dry Gin
¼ Dry Vermouth
¼ Sweet Vermouth
1 Sprig Fresh Mint
Stir well with ice and strain into glass. Serve with a small sprig of Mint or a Cherry.

Cordova
⅔ Dry Gin
⅓ Sweet Vermouth
1 Dash Pernod
1 Teaspoon Cream
Shake well with ice and strain into glass.

Cornell
1 Jigger Dry Gin
3 Dashes Maraschino
1 Egg White
Shake well with ice and strain into glass.

Corpse Reviver No. 2
¼ Dry Gin
¼ Cointreau
¼ Swedish Punch
¼ Lemon Juice
1 Dash Pernod
Shake well with ice and strain into glass.

Cubano
½ Dry Gin
½ Dry Vermouth
4 Drops Kümmel
4 Drops Charbreux
2 Drops Pineapple Syrup
Shake well with ice and strain into glass.

Curaçao
⅙ Gin
⅙ Brandy
⅓ Curaçao
⅓ Orange Juice
Shake well with ice and strain into glass which has had a dash of Orange Bitters.

Damn the Weather
½ Dry Gin
¼ Sweet Vermouth
¼ Orange Juice
3 Dashes Curaçao
Shake well with ice and strain into glass.

Darb
⅓ Dry Gin
⅓ Dry Vermouth
⅓ Apricot Brandy
4 Dashes Lemon Juice
Stir well with ice and strain into glass.

Darby
1 Jigger Dry Gin
⅓ Jigger Lime Juice
⅓ Jigger Grapefruit Juice
1 Teaspoon Powdered Sugar
Shake well with ice and strain into a large cocktail glass. Top with a squirt of Soda and add a Cherry.

Deep Sea
½ Old Tom Gin
½ Dry Vermouth
1 Dash Pernod
1 Dash Orange Bitters
Stir well with ice and strain into glass. Squeeze Lemon Peel over top and serve with an Olive.

Dempsey
½ Dry Gin
½ Calvados or Apple Brandy
2 Dashes Pernod
2 Dashes Grenadine
Stir well with ice and strain into glass.

Depth Charge
½ Dry Gin
½ Lillet
2 Dashes Pernod
Shake well with ice and strain into glass. Squeeze Orange Peel over top.

Derby No. 1
1 Jigger Dry Gin
2 Dashes Peach Bitters
2 Sprigs Fresh Mint
Shake well with ice and strain into glass.

Desert Healer
2 Jiggers Dry Gin
⅓ Jigger Cherry Brandy
Juice of 1 Orange
Shake well with ice and strain into tall glass. Fill with cold Ginger Beer.

Devonia
⅓ Jigger Dry Gin
⅔ Jigger Sparkling Cider
2 Dashes Orange Bitters
Stir lightly with cracked ice and strain into glass.

D.F.
½ Dry Gin
½ Unsweetened Grapefruit Juice
Grenadine to Taste

Stir well with ice and strain into glass.

Diabola
⅓ Dry Gin
⅔ Dubonnet
2 Dashes Orgeat Syrup
Stir well with ice and strain into glass. Serve with a Cherry.

Dick Jr.
⅓ Dry Gin
⅓ Dry Vermouth
⅓ Apricot Brandy
Juice of 1 Lime
Shake well with ice and strain into glass.

Dixie
½ Jigger Dry Gin
¼ Jigger Pernod
¼ Jigger Dry Vermouth
Juice of ¼ Orange
2 Dashes Grenadine
Shake well with ice and strain into glass.

Dodge Special
½ Dry Gin
½ Cointreau
1 Dash Grape Juice
Stir well with ice and strain into glass.

Dolly O'Dare
½ Dry Gin
½ Dry Vermouth
6 Dashes Apricot Brandy
Stir well with ice and strain into glass. Squeeze Orange Peel over top.

D.O.M.
¾ Dry Gin
⅛ Orange Juice
⅛ Benedictine
Shake well with ice and strain into glass.

Douglas
⅔ English Gin
⅓ Dry Vermouth
Stir well with ice and strain into glass. Squeeze Orange or Lemon Peel over top.

Du Barry
⅔ English Gin
⅓ Dry Vermouth
2 Dashes Pernod
1 Dash Angostura Bitters
Stir well with ice and strain into glass. Serve with thin slice of Orange.

Dunhill's Special
⅓ Jigger Dry Gin
⅓ Jigger Sherry
⅓ Jigger Dry Vermouth
1 Tablespoon Curaçao
Stir well with ice and strain into glasses with 2 dashes Pernod and an Olive in each.

Eagle's Dream
¾ Dry Gin
¼ Crème d'Yvette
Juice of ¼ Lemon
1 Egg White
1 Teaspoon Powdered Sugar
Shake well with ice and strain into glass.

Earthquake
⅓ Dry Gin
⅓ Whiskey
⅓ Pernod
Shake well with ice and strain into glass. It's been said by those who know that one of these should be sufficient.

Eclipse
⅓ Dry Gin
⅔ Sloe Gin
Place a Cherry or Ripe Olive in a cocktail glass and add enough Grenadine to cover. Shake the gins with ice and strain slowly into the glass so that they *do not* mix with the Grenadine. Squeeze an Orange Peel over the top.

Eddie Brown
⅔ Dry Gin
⅓ Lillet
2 Dashes Apricot Brandy
Stir well with ice and strain into glass. Squeeze Lemon Peel over top.

Elegant
½ Dry Gin
½ Dry Vermouth
2 Dashes Grand Marnier
Stir well with ice and serve.

Elk
½ Dry Gin
½ Prunelle Brandy
2 Dashes Dry Vermouth
Shake well with ice and strain into glass.

Emerald

1/3 Jigger Dry Gin
1/3 Jigger Green Chartreuse
1/3 Jigger Sweet Vermouth
1 Teaspoon Orange Bitters
Shake well with ice and strain
into glass. Serve with a Cherry
and a twist of Lemon Peel.

Empire

1/2 Dry Gin
1/4 Calvados or Apple Brandy
1/4 Apricot Brandy
Stir well with ice and strain into
glass. Serve with Cherry.

E. Nos

2/3 Dry Gin
1/3 Dry Vermouth
3 Dashes Pernod
Stir well with ice and strain into
glass. Serve with Cherry.

Eton Blazer

3/4 English Gin
1/4 Kirsch
1/2 Tablespoon Powdered Sugar
Juice of 1/2 Lemon
Shake well and strain into large
cocktail glass. Fill with Soda.

Everything But

1/4 Dry Gin
1/4 Whiskey
1/4 Lemon Juice
1/4 Orange Juice
1 Egg
1 Teaspoon Apricot Brandy
1/2 Teaspoon Powdered Sugar
Shake well with ice and strain
into glass.

Fairbanks No. 1

1/3 Dry Gin
1/3 Dry Vermouth
1/3 Apricot Brandy
1 Dash Lemon Juice
1 Dash Grenadine
Stir well with ice and strain into
glass. Serve with Cherry.

Fairbanks No. 2

2/3 Dry Gin
1/3 Dry Vermouth
2 Dashes Orange Bitters
2 Dashes Crème de Noyau
Stir well with ice and strain into
glass. Serve with Cherry.

Fairy Belle

3/4 Dry Gin
1/4 Apricot Brandy
1 Teaspoon Grenadine
1 Egg White
Shake well with ice and strain
into glass.

Fallen Angel

2 Jiggers Dry Gin
Juice of 1 Lemon or Lime
2 Dashes Crème de Menthe
1 Dash Angostura Bitters
Stir well with ice and strain into
glass. Serve with Cherry.

Fall River

1/3 Dry Gin
1/3 Brandy
1/6 White Crème de Menthe
1/6 Maraschino
Shake well with ice and strain
into glass.

Fare-Thee-Well
⅔ Dry Gin
⅓ Dry Vermouth
2 Dashes Sweet Vermouth
6 Dashes Curaçao
Shake well with ice and strain
into glass.

Fascinator
⅔ Dry Gin
⅓ Dry Vermouth
2 Dashes Pernod
1 Sprig Fresh Mint
Shake well with ice and strain
into glass.

Favourite
⅓ Dry Gin
⅓ Dry Vermouth
⅓ Apricot Brandy
1 Dash Lemon Juice
Stir well with ice and strain into
glass. Serve with Cherry.

Fernet Branca
½ Dry Gin
¼ Sweet Vermouth
¼ Fernet Branca
Stir well with ice and strain into
glass. Serve with Cherry.

Fifth Avenue
½ Dry Gin
¼ Sweet Vermouth
¼ Fernet Branca
Stir well with ice and strain into
glass.

Fifty-fifty
½ Dry Gin
½ Dry Vermouth

Stir well with cracked ice and
strain into glass. Serve with
Olive.

Fine and Dandy
½ English Gin
¼ Cointreau
¼ Lemon Juice
1 Dash Angostura Bitters
Stir well with ice and strain into
glass. Serve with Cherry.

Fourth Degree
⅓ Dry Gin
⅓ Dry Vermouth
⅓ Sweet Vermouth
4 Dashes Pernod
Stir well with ice and strain into
glass. Serve with Cherry or a
twist of Lemon Peel.

Frankenjack
⅓ Dry Gin
⅓ Dry Vermouth
⅙ Apricot Brandy
⅙ Cointreau
Stir well with ice and strain into
glass. Serve with Cherry.

French Rose
⅔ Jigger Dry Gin
⅓ Jigger Cherry Brandy
⅓ Jigger Cherry Liqueur
Shake well with ice and strain
into glass.

Froth Blower
1 Jigger English Gin
1 Teaspoon Grenadine
1 Egg White
Shake well with ice and strain
into glass.

Gasper
½ Dry Gin
½ Apricot Brandy
Add if required a very little
Sugar. Shake well with ice and
strain into glass.

Gene Tunney
⅔ English Gin
⅓ Dry Vermouth
1 Dash Orange Juice
1 Dash Lemon Juice
Stir well with ice and strain into
glass. Serve with Cherry.

Gibson
4 Parts Dry Gin or more
1 Part Dry Vermouth or less
Stir well with ice and strain into
glass. Serve with a Pickled Pearl
Onion.

Gilroy
⅓ Dry Gin
⅓ Cherry Brandy
⅙ Dry Vermouth
⅙ Lemon Juice
1 Dash Orange Bitters
Stir well with ice and strain into
glass.

Gimblet
¾ Dry Gin
¼ Lime Juice
Stir well with ice and strain into
glass. Fill with Soda.

Gimlet
½ English Gin
½ Rose's Lime Juice
Stir and serve in same glass. May
be iced if desired.

Gin
1 Jigger Dry Gin
1 Dash Orange Bitters
Stir with cracked ice and strain
into glass. Serve with twist of
Lemon Peel.

Gin and Bitters
2 Jiggers Dry Gin
1 Dash Angostura Bitters
Pour over ice in glass and serve.

Gin and It
½ Dry Gin
½ Sweet Vermouth
Do not ice.

Gin and Sin
¾ Gin
⅛ Orange Juice
⅛ Lemon Juice
1 Dash Grenadine
Shake well with ice and strain
into glass.

Gin Ho or Gin-on-the-Rocks
Fill an Old-Fashioned glass with
cracked ice. Pour on the amount
of Gin desired and serve. A twist
of Lemon Peel may be added.

Gin Rickey (see Rickeys)

Gin Sour
¾ Dry Gin
¼ Lemon Juice
1 Teaspoon Sugar
Shake well with ice.

Gin Stinger
⅔ Dry Gin
⅓ White Crème de Menthe

Shake well with shaved ice and strain into glass.

Golden Clipper
¼ Dry Gin
¼ Light Rum
¼ Peach Brandy
¼ Orange Juice
Shake well with ice and strain into glass.

Golden Dawn
⅔ Jigger Dry Gin
½ Jigger Orange Juice
⅓ Jigger Apricot Brandy
Shake well with ice and strain into glass.

Golden Ermine
½ Dry Gin
⅜ Dry Vermouth
⅛ Sweet Vermouth
Stir with ice and strain into glass.

Golden Gate
¼ Dry Gin
¾ Orange Juice
Place in shaker and shake well without ice. Serve in tall glass.

Golf
⅔ Dry Gin
⅓ Dry Vermouth
2 Dashes Angostura Bitters
Stir well with ice and strain into glass. Serve with Olive.

Grand Royal Clover Club
2 Jiggers Dry Gin
1 Tablespoon Grenadine
Juice of ½ Lemon
1 Egg

Shake well with ice and strain into glass.

Grapefruit
3 Parts Dry Gin
1 Part Grapefruit Juice
Shake well with ice and strain into glass.

Grape Vine
½ Dry Gin
¼ Grape Juice
¼ Lemon Juice
1 Dash Grenadine
Stir well with ice and strain into glass.

Great Secret
⅔ Dry Gin
⅓ Lillet
1 Dash Angostura Bitters
Stir well with ice and strain into glass. Serve with twist of Orange Peel.

Green Dragon No. 1
½ Dry Gin
⅛ Kümmel
¼ Crème de Menthe
⅛ Lemon Juice
4 Dashes Peach Bitters
Shake well with ice and strain into glass.

Guards
⅔ Dry Gin
⅓ Sweet Vermouth
2 Dashes Curaçao
Stir well with ice and strain into glass. Serve with twist of Orange Peel or Cherry.

Gunga Din
¾ Dry Gin
¼ Dry Vermouth
1 Slice Pineapple
Juice of ¼ Orange
Shake well with ice and strain
into glass.

Gypsy
½ English Gin
½ Sweet Vermouth
Stir well with ice and strain into
glass. Serve with Cherry.

Hakam
½ Dry Gin
½ Sweet Vermouth
2 Dashes Curaçao
1 Dash Orange Bitters
Stir well with ice and strain into
glass. Serve with Cherry.

H. and H.
⅔ Dry Gin
⅓ Lillet
2 Dashes Curaçao
Stir well with ice and strain into
glass. Serve with a twist of
Orange Peel.

Hanky-Panky
⅔ Dry Gin
⅓ Sweet Vermouth
2 Dashes Fernet Branca
Stir well with ice and strain into
glass. Serve with twist of Orange
Peel.

Harrovian
2 Jiggers Dry Gin
1 Teaspoon Orange Juice
1 Dash Lemon Juice
1 Dash Angostura Bitters

Stir well with ice and strain into
glass.

Harry's
⅔ Dry Gin
⅓ Sweet Vermouth
1 Dash Pernod
2 Sprigs Fresh Mint
Shake well with ice and strain
into glass. Serve with a Mint Leaf
or two.

Hasty
⅔ Dry Gin
⅓ Dry Vermouth
4 Dashes Grenadine
1 Dash Pernod
Shake well with ice and strain
into glass.

Have a Heart
1 Jigger Dry Gin
½ Jigger Swedish Punch
2 Dashes Grenadine
Juice of ½ Lime
Shake well with shaved ice and
strain into glass. Serve with a
wedge of Pineapple and a
Cherry.

Hawaiian No. 1
1 Jigger Dry Gin
½ Jigger Pineapple Juice
1 Dash Orange Bitters
1 Egg White
Shake well with ice and strain
into glass.

Hawaiian No. 2
4 Parts Dry Gin
1 Part Orange Juice
1 Part Curaçao
Shake well with ice and strain
into glass.

Hoffman House (see Astoria)

Holland House
2/3 Dry Gin
1/3 Dry Vermouth
Juice of 1/4 Lemon
1 Slice Pineapple
4 Dashes Maraschino
Stir well with ice and strain into glass.

Homestead
2/3 Dry Gin
1/3 Sweet Vermouth
1 Slice Orange
Shake well with ice and strain into glass.

Honolulu
1/3 Dry Gin
1/3 Benedictine
1/3 Maraschino
Stir well with ice and strain into glass.

Hotel Plaza
1/3 Dry Gin
1/3 Dry Vermouth
1/3 Sweet Vermouth
1 Slice Pineapple
Shake well with ice and strain into glass.

H.P.W.
1/2 Old Tom Gin
1/2 Dry Vermouth
Stir well with ice and strain into glass. Serve with twist of Orange Peel.

Hugo Special
1 Jigger Dry Gin
1/2 Jigger Sweet Vermouth
2 Slices Orange
1 Slice Pineapple

Place slices of Orange and Pineapple in a mixing glass and muddle well. Add cracked ice, Gin and Vermouth. Shake well and strain into glass.

Hula-Hula
2/3 Dry Gin
1/3 Orange Juice
1 Dash Curaçao
Shake well with ice and strain into glass.

Hurricane
1/3 Dry Gin
1/3 Whiskey
1/3 Crème de Menthe
Juice of 2 Lemons
Shake well with ice and strain into glass.

Ideal
2/3 Dry Gin
1/3 Sweet Vermouth
3 Dashes Maraschino
1 Tablespoon Grapefruit Juice
Shake well with ice and strain into glass.

Imperial
1/2 Dry Gin
1/2 Dry Vermouth
1 Dash Angostura Bitters
1 Dash Maraschino
Stir well with ice and strain into glass. Serve with Olive.

Inca
1/4 Dry Gin
1/4 Sherry
1/4 Dry Vermouth
1/4 Sweet Vermouth
1 Dash Orgeat Syrup
1 Dash Orange Bitters

Stir well with ice and strain into glass.

Income Tax
½ Dry Gin
¼ Dry Vermouth
¼ Sweet Vermouth
1 Dash Angostura Bitters
Juice of ¼ Orange
Stir well with ice and strain into glass.

Jabberwock
⅓ Dry Gin
⅓ Dry Sherry
⅓ Dubonnet
2 Dashes Orange Bitters
Stir well with ice and drain into glass. Squeeze Lemon Peel over top and serve with a Cherry.

Jack Kearns
¾ Dry Gin
¼ Light Rum
4 Dashes Sugar Syrup
1 Dash Lemon Juice
Shake well with ice and strain into glass. This may be made with less Sugar Syrup if desired.

Jack Pine
¾ Dry Gin
¼ Dry Vermouth
1 Slice Pineapple
Juice of ¼ Orange
Shake well with ice and strain into glass.

Jack Sloat
1 Jigger Dry Gin
2 Dashes Dry Vermouth
4 Dashes Sweet Vermouth
3 Slices Pineapple

Shake well with ice and strain into glass.

Jackson
½ Dry Gin
½ Dubonnet
2 Dashes Orange Bitters
Stir well with ice and strain into glass.

Jack Withers
⅓ Dry Gin
⅓ Dry Vermouth
⅓ Sweet Vermouth
Juice of ½ Orange
Stir well with ice and strain.

Jewel
⅓ Dry Gin
⅓ Green Chartreuse
⅓ Sweet Vermouth
1 Dash Orange Bitters
Shake well with ice and strain into glass. Serve with twist of Lemon Peel and, if you want, a Cherry.

Jeyplak
⅔ Dry Gin
⅓ Sweet Vermouth
1 Dash Pernod
Stir well with ice and strain into glass. Twist Lemon Peel over top and serve with a Cherry.

Jimmy Blanc
⅔ Dry Gin
⅓ Lillet
3 Dashes Dubonnet
Stir well with ice and strain into glass. Squeeze Orange Peel over top.

Jockey Club
1½ Jiggers Dry Gin
1 Dash Orange Bitters
1 Dash Angostura Bitters
2 Dashes Crème de Noyau
4 Dashes Lemon Juice
Stir well with ice and strain into glass.

Johnnie Mack
⅔ Sloe Gin
⅓ Curaçao
3 Dashes Pernod
Stir well with ice and strain into glass. Serve with twist of Lemon Peel.

J.O.S.
⅓ Dry Gin
⅓ Dry Vermouth
⅓ Sweet Vermouth
1 Dash Brandy
1 Dash Orange Bitters
1 Dash Lemon or Lime Juice
Stir well with ice and strain into glass. Twist Lemon Peel over top.

Journalist
⅔ Dry Gin
⅙ Dry Vermouth
⅙ Sweet Vermouth
2 Dashes Curaçao
2 Dashes Lemon Juice
1 Dash Angostura Bitters
Stir well with ice and strain into glass.

Judge Jr.
⅓ Dry Gin
⅓ Light Rum
⅓ Lemon Juice
1–3 Dashes Grenadine

Shake well with ice and strain into a glass. Powdered Sugar may be added if more sweetness is desired.

Judgette
⅓ Dry Gin
⅓ Peach Brandy
⅓ Dry Vermouth
1 Dash Lime Juice
Stir well with ice and strain. Serve with Cherry if desired.

K.C.B.
¾ Dry Gin
¼ Kirsch
1 Dash Apricot Brandy
1 Dash Lemon Juice
Stir well with ice and strain into glass. Serve with twist of Lemon Peel.

Kina
½ Dry Gin
¼ Sweet Vermouth
¼ Lillet
Stir well with ice and strain. Serve with Cherry if desired.

Knickerbocker
⅔ Dry Gin
⅓ Dry Vermouth
1 Dash Sweet Vermouth
Stir well with ice and strain into glass. Squeeze Lemon Peel over top.

Knockout
⅓ Dry Gin
⅓ Dry Vermouth
⅓ Pernod
1 Teaspoon White Crème de Menthe

Stir well with ice and strain into glass. Serve with Mint Leaves.

Kup's Indispensable
⅝ Dry Gin
2/8 Dry Vermouth
⅛ Sweet Vermouth
1 Dash Angostura Bitters
Stir well with ice and strain into glass. Serve with twist of Orange Peel.

Lady Finger
½ Dry Gin
¼ Kirsch
¼ Cherry Brandy
Stir well with ice and strain into glass.

Lasky
⅓ Dry Gin
⅓ Swedish Punch
⅓ Grape Juice
Shake well with ice and strain into glass.

Last Round
½ Dry Gin
½ Dry Vermouth
2 Dashes Brandy
2 Dashes Pernod
Stir well with ice and strain into glass.

Leap Frog or London Buck
1 Jigger Dry Gin
Juice of ½ Lemon
Cracked Ice
Place all together in a large cocktail glass and fill with Ginger Ale (or Ginger Beer).

Leap Year
⅔ Dry Gin
⅙ Sweet Vermouth
⅙ Grand Marnier
1 Dash Lemon Juice
Stir well with ice and strain into glass. Squeeze Lemon Peel over top.

Leave It to Me No. 1
½ English Gin
¼ Dry Vermouth
¼ Apricot Brandy
1 Dash Lemon Juice
1 Dash Grenadine
Stir well with ice and strain into glass.

Leave It to Me No. 2
1½ Jiggers Dry Gin
1 Teaspoon Raspberry Syrup
1 Teaspoon Lemon Juice
1 Dash Maraschino
Shake well with ice and strain into glass.

Leo Special
½ Gin
¼ Lime Juice
¼ Cointreau
2 Dashes Pernod
Stir well with ice and strain into glass.

Lilly
⅓ Dry Gin
⅓ Crème de Noyau
⅓ Lillet
1 Dash Lemon Juice
Stir with ice and strain into glass.

Little Devil
⅓ Dry Gin
⅓ Light Rum
⅙ Cointreau
⅙ Lemon Juice
Stir well with ice and strain into glass.

London
1 Jigger English Gin
2 Dashes Maraschino
2 Dashes Sugar Syrup
2 Dashes Orange Bitters
Stir well with ice and strain into glass. Serve with twist of Lemon Peel.

London Buck (see Leap Frog)

Lone Tree
⅓ Dry Gin
⅓ Sweet Vermouth
⅓ Dry Vermouth
2 Dashes Orange Bitters
Stir well with ice and strain into glass. Serve with Cherry.

Lord Suffolk
⅝ Dry Gin
⅛ Cointreau
⅛ Sweet Vermouth
⅛ Maraschino
Stir well with ice and strain into glass. Serve with twist of Lemon Peel.

Loud Speaker
⅜ Dry Gin
⅜ Brandy
⅛ Cointreau
⅛ Lemon Juice
Stir well with ice and strain into glass.

Love
1 Jigger Sloe Gin
1 Egg White
2 Dashes Lemon Juice
2 Dashes Raspberry Syrup
Shake well with ice and strain into glass.

Luigi
½ Dry Gin
½ Dry Vermouth
Juice of ½ Tangerine
1 Dash Cointreau
1 Teaspoon Grenadine
Stir with ice and strain into glass. Serve with Lemon Peel.

Lutkins Special
½ Dry Gin
½ Dry Vermouth
2 Dashes Apricot Brandy
2 Dashes Orange Juice
Stir with ice and strain into glass.

Mabel Berra
½ Jigger Sloe Gin
½ Jigger Swedish Punch
Juice of ½ Lime
Shake well with ice and strain into glass.

Magnolia Blossom
½ Gin
¼ Cream
¼ Lemon Juice
1 Dash Grenadine
Shake quickly with ice and strain into glass.

Mah Jongg
⅔ Dry Gin
⅙ Light Rum
⅙ Cointreau

Stir well with ice and strain into glass. Serve with twist of Lemon Peel.

Maiden's Blush No. 1 or Maiden's Delight
2 Jiggers Dry Gin
4 Dashes Curaçao
4 Dashes Grenadine
1–2 Dashes Lemon Juice
Shake well with ice and strain into glass.

Maiden's Blush No. 2
⅔ Dry Gin
⅓ Pernod
1 Teaspoon Grenadine
Stir well with ice and strain into glass. Serve with twist of Lemon Peel.

Maiden's Prayer No. 1
⅜ Dry Gin
⅜ Cointreau
⅛ Lemon Juice
⅛ Orange Juice
Stir well with ice and strain into glass.

Maiden's Prayer No. 2
⅓ Dry Gin
⅓ Lillet
⅙ Calvados or Apple Brandy
⅙ Apricot Brandy
Stir well with ice and strain into glass.

Manyann
½ Dry Gin
½ Dubonnet
2 Dashes Curaçao
Juice of 1 Lemon
Shake well with ice and strain into glass.

Marguerite
⅔ Gin
⅓ Dry Vermouth
1 Dash Orange Bitters
1 Twist Orange Peel
Stir well with ice and strain into glass. Serve with a Cherry.

Marny
⅔ Dry Gin
⅓ Grand Marnier
Stir well with ice and strain into glass. Serve with a Cherry.

Martinez (for 6)
6 Jiggers Dry Gin
4 Jiggers Dry Vermouth
4 Teaspoons Curaçao or Maraschino
1 Teaspoon Orange Bitters
Shake with ice and strain into glasses. Serve with a twist of Lemon Peel and, if desired, a Cherry.

Martini (dry)
5 or 6 Parts Dry Gin
1 Part Dry Vermouth
Stir with ice and strain into chilled glass. Serve with twist of Lemon Peel or an Olive.

Martini (medium)
2 to 4 Parts Dry Gin
1 Part Dry Vermouth
Stir with ice and strain into chilled glass. Serve with twist of Lemon Peel or an Olive.

Martini (sweet)
3 Parts Dry Gin
½ Part Dry Vermouth
½ Part Sweet Vermouth

Stir with ice and strain into chilled glass. Serve with an Olive. A dash of Orange Bitters may be added.

Martini-on-the-Rocks
Pack an Old-Fashioned glass loosely with ice. Fill with Dry Gin and add a few dashes Dry Vermouth. Stir and serve. A twist of Lemon Peel may be added.

Maurice
½ Dry Gin
¼ Sweet Vermouth
¼ Dry Vermouth
Juice of ¼ Orange
1 Dash of Angostura Bitters
Stir well with ice and strain into glass.

Mayfair
½ Dry Gin
¼ Apricot Brandy
¼ Orange Juice
1 Dash Pimento Dram
Shake well with ice and strain into glass.

McClelland
⅔ Sloe Gin
⅓ Curaçao
1 Dash Orange Bitters
Stir well with ice and strain into glass.

Melon
½ Dry Gin
⅜ Maraschino
⅛ Lemon Juice
Shake well with ice and strain into glass. Serve with a Cherry.

Merry Widow
½ Dry Gin
½ Dry Vermouth
2 Dashes Benedictine
1 Dash Peychaud's Bitters
2 Dashes Pernod
Stir well with ice and strain into glass. Serve with twist of Lemon Peel.

Millionaire No. 1
⅔ Dry Gin
⅓ Pernod
1 Egg White
1 Dash Anisette
Shake well with cracked ice and strain into glass.

Million Dollar
⅔ English Gin
⅓ Sweet Vermouth
1 Tablespoon Pineapple Juice
1 Teaspoon Grenadine
1 Egg White
Shake well with ice and strain into glass.

Minnehaha
½ Dry Gin
¼ Dry Vermouth
¼ Sweet Vermouth
Juice of ¼ Orange
Shake well with ice and strain into glass.

Mint
⅜ Dry Gin
⅛ Crème de Menthe
½ White Wine
Several Sprigs of Mint
Soak the Mint for 2 hours in half the Wine. Add the other ingredients and remaining Wine.

Shake well with ice and strain into glass. Serve with a fresh sprig of Mint in glass.

Mississippi Mule
⅔ Dry Gin
⅙ Lemon Juice
⅙ Crème de Cassis
Stir well with ice and strain into glass.

Mr. Eric Sutton's Gin Blind
6 Parts Gin
3 Parts Curaçao
2 Parts Brandy
1 Dash Orange Bitters
Stir with ice and strain into glass.

Mr. Manhattan
2 Jiggers Dry Gin
4 Dashes Orange Juice
1 Dash Lemon Juice
4 Crushed Mint Leaves
1 Lump Sugar moistened with Water
Shake well with ice and strain into glass.

Modern No. 1
⅔ Sloe Gin
⅓ Scotch Whisky
1 Dash Pernod
1 Dash Orange Bitters
1 Dash Grenadine
Shake well with ice and strain into glass.

Moll
⅓ Dry Gin
⅓ Sloe Gin
⅓ Dry Vermouth
1 Dash Orange Bitters
½ Teaspoon Sugar
Shake and serve.

Monkey Gland
⅔ Dry Gin
⅓ Orange Juice
3 Dashes Benedictine
3 Dashes Grenadine
Stir well with ice and strain into glass.

Monte Carlo Imperial
½ Dry Gin
¼ Lemon Juice
¼ White Crème de Menthe
Shake well with ice and strain into a large cocktail glass. Fill with Champagne.

Moonlight
⅓ Dry Gin
⅙ Kirsch
⅙ Grapefruit Juice
⅓ White Wine
Shake well with ice and strain into glass. Serve with twist of Lemon Peel.

Moonshine
½ Dry Gin
¼ Dry Vermouth
¼ Maraschino
1–2 Drops Pernod
Shake well with ice and strain into glass.

Moulin Rouge
½ Orange Gin
½ Apricot Brandy
3 Dashes Grenadine
Stir well with ice and strain into glass.

Mule Hind Leg
⅕ Dry Gin
⅕ Applejack
⅕ Benedictine
⅕ Maple Syrup
⅕ Apricot Brandy
Stir well with ice and strain into glass.

My Cocktail (same as Marny)

Napoleon
2 Jiggers Dry Gin
1 Dash Dubonnet
1 Dash Curaçao
1 Dash Fernet Branca
Stir well with ice and strain into glass. Squeeze Lemon Peel over top.

Newbury
½ Dry Gin
½ Sweet Vermouth
3 Dashes Curaçao
1 Twist Lemon Peel
1 Twist Orange Peel
Stir well with ice and strain into glass.

Nightmare
⅓ Dry Gin
⅓ Dubonnet
⅙ Cherry Brandy
⅙ Orange Juice
Shake well with ice and strain into glass.

Nineteen
⅓ Dry Gin
⅓ Kirsch
⅓ Dry Vermouth
4 Dashes Sugar Syrup
1 Dash Bitters

Stir well with ice and strain into glass. Serve with Cherry.

Noon
Prepare same as BRONX, adding white of 1 Egg.

No. 6
1 Jigger Dry Gin
½ Jigger Sweet Vermouth
1 Twist Orange Peel
1 Twist Lemon Peel
3 Dashes Curaçao
Shake well with ice and strain into glass. Serve with a Cherry.

Old Etonian
½ Dry Gin
½ Lillet
2 Dashes Orange Bitters
2 Dashes Crème de Noyau
Stir well with ice and strain into glass. Serve with twist of Orange Peel.

Old-Fashioned (with Gin)
1–2 Jiggers Dry Gin
1 Slice Lemon Peel
½ Piece Lump Sugar
1 Dash Angostura Bitters
Place Sugar in bottom of Old-Fashioned glass and sprinkle with Bitters. Add Lemon and ice cubes and fill with Gin as desired. Stir and serve.

Olivette
1½ Jiggers English Gin
2 Dashes Sugar Syrup
2 Dashes Orange Bitters
Stir with ice and strain into glass. Serve with twist of Lemon Peel, and an Olive if desired.

One Exciting Night
⅓ English Gin
⅓ Dry Vermouth
⅓ Sweet Vermouth
1 Dash Orange Juice
Shake well with ice and strain
into glass. Twist Lemon Peel over
top. Glasses should be frosted
with Powdered Sugar.

One of Mine
½ Dry Gin
¼ Dry Vermouth
¼ Sweet Vermouth
Juice of ¼ Orange
1 Dash Bitters
Stir well with ice and strain into
glass.

Opal
½ Dry Gin
⅓ Orange Juice
⅙ Cointreau
¼ Teaspoon Powdered Sugar
Shake well with ice and strain
into glass. A little Orange Flower
Water may be added, if available.

Opera
⅔ Dry Gin
⅙ Dubonnet
⅙ Maraschino
Stir well with ice and strain into
glass. Squeeze Orange Peel over
top.

Orange (for 6)
⅖ Gin
⅖ Orange Juice
⅕ Dry Vermouth
2 Dashes Orange Bitters
2 Teaspoons Powdered Sugar
Combine in shaker and place on
ice for half an hour. Then shake

with ice and strain into glasses.
Serve with twists of Orange Peel.

Orange Bloom
½ Dry Gin
¼ Sweet Vermouth
¼ Cointreau
Stir with ice and strain into glass.
Serve with a Cherry.

Orange Blossom
2–3 Jiggers Dry Gin
1 Jigger Orange Juice
Stir well with cracked ice and
strain into glass. Powdered Sugar
or Sugar Syrup may be added if
desired.

Orange Martini
½ Gin
¼ Dry Vermouth
¼ Sweet Vermouth
1 Orange Rind, grated carefully.
Steep the Orange Rind for two
hours in the combined liquors.
Shake well with ice and strain
into glasses in each of which has
been put a dash of Orange Bitters.

Pall Mall
⅓ English Gin
⅓ Dry Vermouth
⅓ Sweet Vermouth
1 Teaspoon White Crème de
Menthe
1 Dash Orange Bitters
Stir well with ice and strain.

Paradise
⅓ Dry Gin
⅓ Apricot Brandy
⅓ Orange or Lemon Juice
Stir well with ice and strain.

Parisian
⅓ Dry Gin
⅓ Dry Vermouth
⅓ Crème de Cassis
Stir well with ice and strain.

Pat's Special
⅓ Dry Gin
⅓ Sherry
⅓ Quinquina
2 Dashes Crème de Cassis
2 Dashes Apricot Brandy
Shake well with ice and strain
into glasses. Serve with Cherry
and a piece of Orange Peel in
each.

Peggy
⅔ Dry Gin
⅓ Dry Vermouth
1 Dash Pernod
1 Dash Dubonnet
Stir well with ice and strain into
glass.

Pegu Club
⅔ Dry Gin
⅓ Curaçao
1 Dash Orange Bitters
1 Dash Angostura Bitters
1 Teaspoon Lime Juice
Shake well with ice and strain
into glass.

Perfect
⅓ Dry Gin
⅓ Dry Vermouth
⅓ Sweet Vermouth
Stir well with ice and strain into
glass.

Peter Pan
¼ Dry Gin
¼ Dry Vermouth
¼ Orange Juice
¼ Peach Brandy
Shake well with ice and strain
into glass.

Peto
½ English Gin
¼ Sweet Vermouth
¼ Dry Vermouth
Juice of ¼ Orange
2 Dashes Maraschino
Stir well with ice and strain into
glass.

Piccadilly
⅔ Dry Gin
⅓ Dry Vermouth
1 Dash Pernod
1 Dash Grenadine
Stir well with ice and strain into
glass.

Ping-Pong
½ Sloe Gin
½ Crème d'Yvette
Juice of ¼ Lemon
Shake well with ice and strain
into glass.

Ping-Pong Special
½ Sloe Gin
½ Sweet Vermouth
1 Teaspoon Angostura Bitters
2 Teaspoons Curaçao
Stir well with ice and strain into
glass. Serve with a Cherry and
a twist of Lemon Peel.

Pink Baby
½ Dry Gin
¼ Grenadine
¼ Sirop de Citron
1 Egg White
Shake well with ice and strain
into glass.

Pink Gin (see Gin and Bitters)

Pink Lady No. 1
1 Jigger Dry Gin
1 Jigger Apple Brandy
1 Tablespoon Grenadine
1 Jigger Lemon Juice
1 Egg White
Shake well with ice and strain
into glass.

Pink Lady No. 2
1 Jigger Gin
½ Jigger Lemon Juice
1 Tablespoon Grenadine
1 Egg White
Shake well and pour into chilled
glass.

Pink Rose
⅔ Jigger Dry Gin
1 Teaspoon Grenadine
1 Teaspoon Lemon Juice
1 Teaspoon Cream
1 Egg White
Shake well with ice and strain
into glass.

Pinky
½ Dry Gin
½ Grenadine
1 Egg White
Shake well with cracked ice and
strain.

Plaza (see Hotel Plaza)

Pollyanna
1 Jigger Dry Gin
¼ Jigger Grenadine
¼ Jigger Sweet Vermouth
3 Slices Orange
3 Slices Pineapple
Muddle the Orange and
Pineapple slices in the bottom of
a shaker. Add ice and the other
ingredients. Shake well and strain
into glass.

Polo No. 1
⅓ Dry Gin
⅓ Dry Vermouth
⅓ Sweet Vermouth
Juice of ⅓ Lime
Shake well with ice and strain
into glass.

Polo No. 2
⅔ English Gin
⅙ Grapefruit Juice
⅙ Orange Juice
Shake well with ice and strain
into glass.

Polly or Poppy
⅔ Dry Gin
⅓ Crème de Cacao
Stir well with ice and strain into
glass.

Pooh-Bah
⅓ Dry Gin
⅓ Light Rum
⅓ Swedish Punch
1 Dash Apricot Brandy
Stir well with ice and strain into
glass.

Princess Mary
1/3 Dry Gin
1/3 Crème de Cacao
1/3 Cream
Shake well with ice and strain
into glass.

Prince's Smile
1/2 Dry Gin
1/4 Calvados or Apple Brandy
1/4 Apricot Brandy
1 Dash Lemon Juice
Stir well with ice and strain into
glass.

Princeton
1 Jigger Dry Gin
1/3 Jigger Port
2 Dashes Orange Bitters
Stir with ice and strain into glass.
Serve with a twist of Lemon Peel.

Prohibition
1/2 Gin
1/2 Lillet
2 Dashes Orange Juice
1 Dash Apricot Brandy
Shake well with ice and strain
into glass. Squeeze Lemon Peel
over top.

Queen
2/3 Dry Gin
1/3 Sweet Vermouth
3 Slices Pineapple
Muddle Pineapple slices in
shaker. Add other ingredients
with ice. Stir well and strain into
glass.

Queen Elizabeth
1/2 Dry Gin
1/4 Cointreau
1/4 Lemon Juice
1 Dash Pernod
Stir well with ice and strain into
glass.

Queen's
1/2 Dry Gin
1/4 Dry Vermouth
1/4 Sweet Vermouth
1/2 Slice Pineapple
Muddle the Pineapple in shaker.
Add ice and other ingredients
and stir. Strain into glass.

R.A.C. Special
1/2 Dry Gin
1/4 Sweet Vermouth
1/4 Dry Vermouth
2 Dashes Orange Bitters
Stir well with ice and strain into
glass. Squeeze Orange Peel over
top.

Racquet Club
2/3 English Gin
1/3 Dry Vermouth
1 Dash Orange Bitters
Stir well with ice and strain into
glass.

Raspberry (for 6)
4 Jiggers Dry Gin
1 Jigger Kirsch
4 Jiggers Dry White Wine
1 Cup Bruised Fresh Raspberries
Soak the Raspberries in the Gin
for 2 hours. Strain and add other
ingredients. Shake well with ice
and strain into glasses. Serve with
a fresh Raspberry in each.

Red Baron
1 Jigger Gin
½ Jigger Grenadine
1 Jigger Orange Juice
½ Jigger Lime Juice
Pour over ice in Old-Fashioned
glass.

Resolute
½ Dry Gin
¼ Apricot Brandy
¼ Lemon Juice
Stir well with ice and strain into
glass.

Retreat from Moscow
½ Dry Gin
¼ Kümmel
¼ Lemon Juice
Shake well with ice and strain
into glass.

Richmond
⅔ English Gin
⅓ Lillet
Stir well with ice and strain into
glass. Squeeze Lemon Peel over
top.

Riveredge
½ Dry Gin
¼ Dry Vermouth
¼ Water
4 Inch-wide Strips Orange Peel
Place all the ingredients,
including the peel, in an electric
mixer, and mix for two minutes.
Strain into glasses and serve with
a sliver of Orange Peel in each.

Roc-A-Coe
½ Dry Gin
½ Sherry

Stir well with ice and strain into
glass. Serve with a Cherry.

Rolls Royce
½ Dry Gin
¼ Dry Vermouth
¼ Sweet Vermouth
1 or 2 Dashes Benedictine
Stir well with ice and strain into
glass.

Rosa
1 Jigger Dry Gin
⅓ Jigger Kirsch
⅓ Jigger Apricot Brandy
Stir well with ice and strain into
glass.

Rose (English) No. 1
½ Dry Gin
¼ Dry Vermouth
¼ Apricot Brandy
4 Dashes Grenadine
1 Dash Lemon Juice
Shake well with ice and strain
into glass. Frost rim of glass with
Powdered Sugar.

Rose (French) No. 2
½ Dry Gin
¼ Dry Vermouth
¼ Cherry Brandy
Stir well with ice and strain into
glass. (Kirsch may be used
instead of the Dry Vermouth.)

Roselyn
⅔ Dry Gin
⅓ Dry Vermouth
2 Dashes Grenadine
Stir well with ice and strain into
glass. Squeeze Lemon Peel over
top.

Rosington
2/3 Dry Gin
1/3 Sweet Vermouth
Stir well with ice and strain into glass. Squeeze Orange Peel over top.

Royal No. 1
1/3 Dry Gin
1/3 Dry Vermouth
1/3 Cherry Brandy
Stir well with ice and strain.

Royal No. 2
Prepare same as ROYAL NO. 1, adding 1 dash Maraschino. Serve with a Cherry.

Royal Clover Club
2 Jiggers Gin
Juice of 1/2 Lemon
1 Tablespoon Grenadine
1 Egg Yolk
Shake well with ice and strain into glass.

Royal Smile
1/2 Dry Gin
1/2 Grenadine
2 Dashes Lemon Juice
Stir well with ice and strain into glass.

Russian
1/3 Dry Gin
1/3 Vodka
1/3 Crème de Cacao
Stir well with ice and strain into glass.

Salome
1/3 Dry Gin
1/3 Dry Vermouth
1/3 Dubonnet

Stir well with ice and strain into glass.

Sandmartin
1/2 Dry Gin
1/2 Sweet Vermouth
1 Teaspoon Green Chartreuse
Stir well with ice and strain into glass.

Satan's Whiskers—Straight
1/3 Dry Gin
1/5 Dry Vermouth
1/5 Sweet Vermouth
1/5 Orange Juice
1/10 Grand Marnier
1/10 Orange Bitters
Stir well with ice and strain into glass.

Satan's Whiskers—Curled
Substitute Curaçao for the Grand Marnier in the foregoing recipe.

Savoy Hotel Special No. 1
2/3 Dry Gin
1/3 Dry Vermouth
2 Dashes Grenadine
1 Dash Pernod
Stir well with ice and strain into glass. Squeeze Lemon Peel over top.

Savoy Hotel Special No. 2
2/3 English Gin
1/3 Dry Vermouth
2 Dashes Dubonnet
Stir well with ice and strain into glass. Squeeze Orange Peel over top.

Savoy Tango
½ Sloe Gin
½ Applejack or Calvados
Shake well with ice and strain
into glass.

Self-Starter
½ Dry Gin
⅜ Lillet
⅛ Apricot Brandy
2 Dashes Pernod
Stir well with ice and strain into
glass.

Sensation
¾ Dry Gin
¼ Lemon Juice
3 Dashes Maraschino
3 Sprigs Fresh Mint
Shake well with ice and strain
into glass.

Seventh Heaven No. 1
½ Dry Gin
½ Dubonnet
2 Dashes Maraschino
1 Dash Angostura Bitters
Stir well with ice and strain into
glass. Squeeze Orange Peel on
top. Serve with a Cherry.

Seventh Heaven No. 2
¾ Dry Gin
¼ Maraschino
1 Tablespoon Grapefruit Juice
Stir well with ice and strain into
glass. Serve with a sprig of fresh
Mint.

Seventh Regiment
⅔ Dry Gin
⅓ Sweet Vermouth
2 Twists of Thin Lemon Peel

Stir well with ice and strain into
glass.

Shriner
½ Jigger Sloe Gin
½ Jigger Brandy
2 Dashes Sugar Syrup
2 Dashes Peychaud's Bitters
Stir well with ice and strain into
glass. Serve with a twist of
Lemon Peel.

Silver
½ Dry Gin
½ Dry Vermouth
2 Dashes Orange Bitters
2 Dashes Maraschino
Stir well with ice and strain into
glass. Serve with twist of Lemon
Peel.

Silver Bullet
½ Dry Gin
¼ Kümmel
¼ Lemon Juice
Stir well with ice and strain into
glass.

Silver King
1 Jigger Dry Gin
Juice of ½ Lemon
2 Dashes Orange Bitters
2 Dashes Sugar Syrup
1 Egg White
Shake well with ice and strain
into glass.

Silver Stallion
½ Dry Gin
½ Vanilla Ice Cream
Juice of ½ Lime
Juice of ½ Lemon

Shake with small amount of shaved ice. Strain into glass and fill with Soda Water.

Silver Streak
½ Dry Gin
½ Kümmel
Stir well with ice and strain into glass.

Sloeberry
2 Jiggers Sloe Gin
1 Dash Orange Bitters
1 Dash Angostura Bitters
Stir well with ice and strain into glass.

Sloe Gin
1 Jigger Sloe Gin
1 Dash Orange Bitters
1 Dash Dry Vermouth
Stir well with ice and strain into glass.

Smiler
½ Dry Gin
¼ Dry Vermouth
¼ Sweet Vermouth
1 Dash Angostura Bitters
1 Dash Orange Bitters
Stir well with ice and strain into glass.

Snapper (see Gin Stinger)

Snicker
⅔ Dry Gin
⅓ Dry Vermouth
2 Dashes Maraschino
1 Dash Orange Bitters
1 Teaspoon Sugar Syrup
1 Egg White

Shake well with ice and strain into glass.

Snowball
½ Dry Gin
⅛ Crème de Menthe
⅛ Anisette
⅛ Cream
Shake well with ice and strain into glass.

Snyder
2 Dashes Curaçao
⅔ Dry Gin
⅓ Dry Vermouth
Stir well with ice and strain into glass. Serve with ice cube and twist of Orange Peel.

Some Moth
⅔ English Gin
⅓ Dry Vermouth
2 Dashes Pernod
Shake well with ice and strain into glass. Serve with a Pickled Pearl Onion.

Sonza's Wilson
½ Gin
½ Cherry Brandy
4 Dashes of Lemon or Lime Juice
4 Dashes Grenadine
Stir well with ice and strain into glass.

So-So
⅓ Dry Gin
⅓ Sweet Vermouth
⅙ Calvados or Apple Brandy
⅙ Grenadine
Stir well with ice and strain into glass.

Sour Kisses
⅔ Dry Gin
⅓ Dry Vermouth
1 Egg White
Shake well with ice and strain
into glass.

Southern Bride
⅔ Dry Gin
⅓ Grapefruit Juice
3 Dashes Maraschino
Shake well with ice and strain
into glass.

Southern Gin
2 Jiggers Dry Gin
2 Dashes Orange Bitters
2 Dashes Curaçao
Shake well with ice and strain
into glass. Serve with a twist of
Lemon Peel.

South Side
2 Jiggers Dry Gin
Juice of ½ Lemon
½ Tablespoon Powdered Sugar
2 Sprigs of Fresh Mint
Shake well with ice and strain
into glass. Add a dash of Soda
Water if desired.

Spencer
⅔ Dry Gin
⅓ Apricot Brandy
1 Dash Orange Juice
1 Dash Angostura Bitters
Stir well with ice and strain into
glass. Squeeze Orange Peel over
top and serve with a Cherry.

Spring (for 6)
6 Jiggers Dry Gin
2 Jiggers Quinquina
2 Jiggers Benedictine
1 Dash Bitters
Shake well with ice and strain
into glasses. Serve with an Olive.

Spring Feeling
½ English Gin
¼ Green Chartreuse
¼ Lemon Juice
Stir well with ice and strain into
glass.

Stanley
⅓ Gin
⅓ Rum
⅙ Grenadine
⅙ Lemon Juice
Stir well with ice and strain into
glass.

Star No. 2
½ Dry Gin
½ Calvados or Apple Brandy
1 Dash Dry Vermouth
1 Dash Sweet Vermouth
1 Teaspoon Grapefruit Juice
Stir well with ice and strain into
glass.

Straight Law
⅓ Dry Gin
⅔ Dry Sherry
Shake well with ice and strain
into glass.

Strike's Off
½ Gin
¼ Swedish Punch
¼ Lemon Juice

Stir well with ice and strain into glass.

Submarine
½ Dry Gin
¼ Dubonnet
¼ Dry Vermouth
1 Dash Bitters
Stir well with ice and strain.

Summer Time
¾ Gin
¼ Sirop de Citron
Stir well with ice and strain into glass. Fill up with Soda Water.

Sunshine No. 1
⅔ Dry Gin
⅓ Sweet Vermouth
1 Dash Angostura Bitters
1 Lump of Ice
Stir together and strain into glass. Squeeze Orange Peel over top.

Sweet Patootie
½ Dry Gin
¼ Cointreau
¼ Orange Juice
Stir well with ice and strain into glass.

Swizzles
2 Jiggers Gin
Juice of 1 Lime
1 Dash Angostura Bitters
1 Teaspoon Sugar
Stir with swizzle stick until it foams. Add 1 lump of ice.

Tango
½ Dry Gin
¼ Sweet Vermouth
¼ Dry Vermouth
2 Dashes Curaçao
Juice of ¼ Orange
Stir well with ice and strain into glass.

Third Degree
⅔ English Gin
⅓ Dry Vermouth
4 Dashes Pernod
Stir well with ice and strain into glass.

Three Stripes
⅔ Dry Gin
⅓ Dry Vermouth
3 Slices Orange
Shake well with ice and strain into glass.

Thunderclap
⅓ Gin
⅓ Whiskey
⅓ Brandy
Shake well with ice and strain into glass. Drink this at your own risk!

Tidbit
½ Dry Gin
½ Vanilla Ice Cream
1 Dash Sherry
Shake well till thoroughly blended. If you think anything else is necessary, serve with a Cherry.

Tipperary No. 1

1/3 Dry Gin
1/3 Dry Vermouth
1/6 Orange Juice
1/6 Grenadine
2 Sprigs of Mint
Shake well with ice and strain into glass.

Transvaal

1/2 Gin
1/2 Dubonnet
3 Dashes Orange Bitters
Stir well with ice and strain into glass.

Trilby No. 1

1/2 Gin
1/2 Sweet Vermouth
2 Dashes Orange Bitters
Shake well with ice and strain into a glass. Float a little Crème d'Yvette on top and serve.

Trinity

1/3 Dry Gin
1/3 Dry Vermouth
1/3 Sweet Vermouth
Stir well with ice and strain into glass.

Turf or Tuxedo No. 1

1/2 Gin
1/2 Dry Vermouth
2 Dashes Pernod
1 Piece Lemon Peel
Stir well with ice and strain into glass.

Tuxedo No. 2

1/2 Dry Gin
1/2 Dry Vermouth
2 Dashes Orange Bitters
1 Dash Pernod
1 Dash Maraschino
Stir well with ice and strain into glass. Add a Cherry and squeeze Lemon Peel over the top.

Twin Six

1 Jigger Gin
1/2 Jigger Sweet Vermouth
1 Dash Grenadine
3 Slices Orange
1 Egg White
Shake well with ice and strain into glass.

Ulanda

2/3 Dry Gin
1/3 Cointreau
1 Dash Pernod
Stir well with ice and strain into glass.

Union Jack

2/3 Dry Gin
1/3 Crème d'Yvette
Stir well with ice and strain into glass.

Up in the Air

1 Jigger Dry Gin
1/3 Jigger Lemon Juice
2 Teaspoons Maraschino
Shake well with ice and strain into glass. If you go for such fancies, a dash of Blue Vegetable Extract may be added.

Van

2/3 Dry Gin
1/3 Dry Vermouth
2 Dashes Grand Marnier
Stir well with ice and strain into glass.

Velocity

1/3 Dry Gin
2/3 Sweet Vermouth
1 Slice Orange
Shake well with ice and strain into glass.

Victor

1/4 Dry Gin
1/4 Brandy
1/2 Sweet Vermouth
Stir well with ice and strain into glass.

Vie Rose

1/3 Dry Gin
1/3 Kirsch
1/6 Lemon Juice
1/6 Grenadine
Shake well with ice and strain into glass.

Virgin

1/3 Dry Gin
1/3 Forbidden Fruit Liqueur
1/3 White Crème de Menthe
Stir well with ice and strain into glass.

Waldorf

1/4 Dry Gin
1/2 Swedish Punch
Juice of 1/4 Lemon or Lime
Shake well with ice and strain into glass.

Wallick

1/2 Dry Gin
1/2 Dry Vermouth
3 Dashes Orange Flower Water
Stir well with ice and strain into glass. Curaçao may be used in place of the Orange Flower Water.

Wardays

1/3 Dry Gin
1/3 Sweet Vermouth
1/3 Calvados or Apple Brandy
1 Teaspoon Yellow Chartreuse
Shake well with ice and strain into glass.

Ward Eight No. 1

Prepare same as MARTINI (dry), adding 2 twists of Orange Peel.

Wax

2 Jiggers English Gin
3 Dashes Orange Bitters
Stir well with ice and strain into glass.

Webster

1/2 English Gin
1/4 Dry Vermouth
1/8 Apricot Brandy
1/8 Lime Juice
Shake well with ice and strain into glass.

Wedding Belle

1/3 Dry Gin
1/3 Dubonnet
1/6 Orange Juice
1/6 Cherry Brandy
Shake well with ice and strain into glass.

Weesuer Special

¼ Dry Gin
¼ Curaçao
¼ Dry Vermouth
¼ Sweet Vermouth
4 Dashes Pernod
Stir well with ice and strain into glass.

Welcome Stranger

⅙ Dry Gin
⅙ Swedish Punch
⅙ Brandy
⅙ Grenadine
⅙ Lemon Juice
⅙ Orange Juice
Shake well with ice and strain into glass.

Wellington

1 Jigger Dry Gin
2 Dashes Swedish Punch
2 Dashes Cherry Brandy
Juice of ½ Lime
Stir well with ice and strain into glass.

Wembly No. 1

⅔ Dry Gin
⅓ Dry Vermouth
2–3 Dashes Calvados or Apple Brandy
Stir well with ice and strain into glass.

Westbrook

⅗ Dry Gin
⅕ Sweet Vermouth
⅕ Bourbon Whiskey
½ Teaspoon Powdered Sugar
Shake well with ice and strain into glass.

Western Rose

½ Dry Gin
¼ Dry Vermouth
¼ Apricot Brandy
1 Dash Lemon Juice
Stir well with ice and strain into glass.

West Indian

2 Jiggers English Gin
4 Dashes Angostura Bitters
1 Teaspoon Sugar
1 Teaspoon Lemon Juice
2 Cubes Ice
Combine, stir and serve in the same glass.

White

2 Jiggers Dry Gin
2 Teaspoons Anisette
2 Dashes Orange Bitters
Stir well with ice and strain into glass. Squeeze Lemon Peel over top.

White Baby

½ Dry Gin
¼ Cointreau
¼ Sirop de Citron
Stir well with ice and strain into glass.

White Cargo

½ Dry Gin
½ Vanilla Ice Cream
No ice is necessary. Shake together till blended and pour into glass.

White Lady

½ Dry Gin
¼ Cointreau
¼ Lemon Juice

Shake well with ice and strain into glass.

White Lily
1/3 Dry Gin
1/3 Light Rum
1/3 Cointreau
1 Dash Pernod
Stir well with ice and strain into glass.

White Plush
2 Jiggers Dry Gin
2/3 Jigger Maraschino
1 Cup Milk
Shake well with ice and strain into glass.

White Rose
1 Jigger Dry Gin
Juice of 1/4 Orange
Juice of 1 Lime
1/2 Jigger Maraschino
1 Egg White
Shake well with ice and strain into glass.

White Way
2/3 Dry Gin
1/3 White Crème de Menthe
Shake well with ice and strain into glass. This is similar to the
GIN STINGER.

White Wings (same as White Way)

Whizz-Doodle
1/4 Dry Gin
1/4 Crème de Cacao
1/4 Scotch Whisky
1/4 Cream

Shake well with ice and strain into glass.

Why Not
1/3 Dry Gin
1/3 Dry Vermouth
1/2 Apricot Brandy
1 Dash Lemon Juice
Shake well with ice and strain into glass.

Wild Oat
3/4 Dry Gin
1/4 Kirsch
1 Dash Lemon Juice
1 Dash Apricot Brandy
Shake well with ice and strain into glass.

Will Rogers
1/2 English Gin
1/4 Dry Vermouth
1/4 Orange Juice
4 Dashes Curaçao
Shake well with ice and strain into glass.

Wilson Special
2 Jiggers Dry Gin
2 Dashes Dry Vermouth
2 Slices Orange
Shake well with ice and strain into glass.

Xanthia
1/3 Dry Gin
1/3 Yellow Chartreuse
1/3 Cherry Brandy
Stir well with ice and strain into glass.

Yachting Club
⅔ Holland Gin
⅓ Dry Vermouth
2 Dashes Sugar Syrup
2 Dashes Peychaud's Bitters
1 Dash Pernod
Stir well with ice and strain into glass.

Yale
1 Jigger Dry Gin
½ Jigger Dry Vermouth
3 Dashes Orange Bitters
2 Dashes Sugar Syrup
1 Dash Maraschino
Stir well with ice and strain into glass.

Yellow Daisy (for 6)
4 Jiggers Dry Gin
4 Jiggers Dry Vermouth
2 Jiggers Grand Marnier
1 Dash Pernod
Shake well with ice and strain into glasses. Serve with a Cherry.

Yellow Rattler
¼ Dry Gin
¼ Dry Vermouth
¼ Sweet Vermouth
¼ Orange Juice
Shake well with ice and strain into glass with small crushed Pickled Onion.

Yokohama
⅓ Dry Gin
⅙ Vodka
⅓ Orange Juice
⅙ Grenadine
1 Dash Pernod
Stir well with ice and strain into glass.

Yolanda
¼ Dry Gin
¼ Brandy
½ Sweet Vermouth
1 Dash Grenadine
1 Dash Pernod
Stir well with ice and strain into glass.

Zaza
1 Jigger Dry Gin
1 Jigger Dubonnet
1 Twist Orange Peel
Stir well with ice and strain into glass.

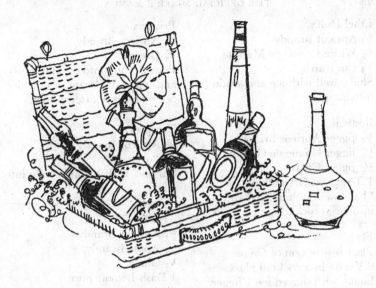

COCKTAILS—LIQUEUR BASES

Many of the following cocktails call for equal quantities of Liqueurs. Hence their listing is arbitrary.

APRICOT BRANDY

After Dinner
½ Apricot Brandy
½ Curaçao
Juice of 1 Lime, with twist of Peel
Shake well with ice and strain into glass.

After Supper
½ Apricot Brandy
½ Curaçao
2 Dashes Lemon Juice
Stir well with ice and strain into glass.

Apricot
½ Apricot Brandy
¼ Orange Juice
¼ Lemon Juice
1 Dash Dry Gin
Shake well with ice and strain into glass.

Babbie's Special
⅔ Apricot Brandy
⅓ Cream
1 Dash Gin
Shake well with ice and strain into glass.

Culross
⅓ Apricot Brandy
⅓ Light Rum
⅓ Lillet
Juice of ¼ Lemon
Stir well with ice and strain into glass.

Ethel Duffy

⅓ Apricot Brandy
⅓ White Crème de Menthe
⅓ Curaçao
Shake well with ice and strain into glass.

Festival

½ Jigger Apricot Brandy
½ Jigger Crème de Cacao
½ Jigger Cream
1 Teaspoon Grenadine
Shake well with ice and strain into large cocktail glass.

Flag

Place a teaspoon of Crème d'Yvette in a cocktail glass. Shake with shaved ice 1 jigger Apricot Brandy and 4 dashes Curaçao. Pour into glass carefully so as not to mix. Top with Claret.

Havana

½ Apricot Brandy
¼ Swedish Punch
¼ Dry Gin
1 Dash Lemon Juice
Stir well with ice and strain into glass.

Hop Toad

¾ Apricot Brandy
¼ Lemon Juice
Stir well with ice and strain into glass.

Mother Sherman

1½ Jiggers Apricot Brandy
⅔ Jigger Orange Juice
4 Dashes Orange Bitters
Shake well with shaved ice and strain into large cocktail glass.

Princess

¾ Apricot Brandy
¼ Cream
Pour Brandy into cocktail glass and top with Cream so they do not mix. Serve after dinner.

Tempter

½ Apricot Brandy
½ Port
Stir well with ice and strain into glass.

Tender

¼ Apricot Brandy
¼ Apple Brandy
½ Gin
1 Dash Lemon Juice
Shake well with ice and strain into glass.

Valencia

⅔ Apricot Brandy
⅓ Orange Juice
4 Dashes Orange Bitters
Stir well with ice and strain into glass. This may also be poured into a tall glass and filled with Champagne.

Yellow Parrot

⅓ Apricot Brandy
⅓ Yellow Chartreuse
⅓ Pernod
Shake well with ice and strain into glass.

BENEDICTINE

B. and B.

½ Benedictine
½ Brandy

Serve in a liqueur glass or iced in a cocktail glass. This is an after-dinner drink.

Benedictine
Place in a shaker with ice 2 jiggers Benedictine and a dash of Angostura Bitters. Shake slightly and strain into a cocktail glass, the rim of which has been rubbed with a slice of Lemon and then dipped into Powdered Sugar. Serve with a Maraschino Cherry.

Benedictine Cocktail
Rub the rim of a cocktail glass with Lemon and dip in Powdered Sugar. Place a Cherry in and add the following mixture: Combine in a shaker, with ice, 1 dash Angostura Bitters and 1 jigger Benedictine. Shake slightly and strain into prepared glass.

Benedictine Frappé
Fill a large cocktail glass with shaved ice and fill with Benedictine. Serve after dinner with straws.

Widow's Dream
2 Jiggers Benedictine
1 Egg
1 Jigger Cream
Shake well with ice and strain into glass.

BLACKBERRY

Windy Corner
2 Jiggers Blackberry Brandy
Shake well with shaved ice and serve with a grating of Nutmeg.

You Never Know
2 Jiggers Blackberry Brandy
1 Jigger White Crème de Menthe
1 Grating of Nutmeg
Stir well with ice and strain into glass.

CHARTREUSE

Chocolate No. 2
1 Jigger Yellow Chartreuse
1 Jigger Maraschino
1 Egg
1 Teaspoon Powdered Sugar
Shake well with ice and strain into glass.

Golden Slipper
½ Jigger Yellow Chartreuse
½ Jigger Eau de Vie Danzig
1 Egg Yolk
Shake well with ice and strain into glass.

Green Dragon No. 2
½ Green Chartreuse
½ Brandy
Stir with shaved ice and strain into glass.

H-Bomb
¼ Yellow Chartreuse
¼ Green Chartreuse
¼ Brandy
¼ Bourbon Whiskey
Shake well with ice and strain into glass.

Harvey Wallbanger
(see under Vodka)

Rainbow

1/7 Yellow Chartreuse
1/7 Green Chartreuse
1/7 Crème de Cacao
1/7 Crème de Violette
1/7 Maraschino
1/7 Benedictine
1/7 Brandy

Pour ingredients carefully into large liqueur glass so that they do not mix. Serve only after dinner. This is a version of Pousse Café.

St. Germain

2 Jiggers Green Chartreuse
1 Egg White
Juice of ½ Lemon or ¼ Grapefruit

Shake well with ice and strain into glass.

Stars and Stripes

⅓ Green Chartreuse
⅓ Maraschino
⅓ Crème de Cassis

Pour carefully into liqueur glass so that ingredients do not mix. Serve after dinner.

Union Jack

⅓ Green Chartreuse
⅓ Maraschino
⅓ Grenadine

Pour ingredients carefully into liqueur glass so that they do not mix. Serve after dinner.

CHERRY BRANDY

Bulldog

1 Jigger Cherry Brandy
½ Jigger Light Rum
Juice of ½ Lime

Shake well with ice and strain into glass.

Merry Widow

½ Cherry Brandy
½ Maraschino

Shake well with ice and serve with a Cherry.

Purple Bunny

1 Jigger Cherry Brandy
⅓ Jigger Crème de Cacao
⅔ Jigger Cream

Shake well with ice and strain into large cocktail glass.

Wallick's

½ Cherry Brandy
½ White Curaçao

Shake well with ice and strain into glass.

COINTREAU

Albertine

⅓ Cointreau
⅓ Yellow Chartreuse
⅓ Kirsch
1 Dash Maraschino

Shake well with ice and strain into glass.

Blanche

⅓ Cointreau
⅓ Anisette
⅓ White Curaçao

Shake well with ice and strain into glass.

Broadway Smile

⅓ Cointreau
⅓ Swedish Punch
⅓ Crème de Cassis

Pour carefully into liqueur glass so that ingredients do not mix. Serve after dinner.

Bud's Special
⅔ Cointreau
⅓ Cream
1 Dash Angostura Bitters
Stir well with ice and strain into glass.

Lollypop (for 6)
2 Jiggers Cointreau
2 Jiggers Chartreuse
2 Jiggers Kirsch
1 Dash Maraschino
Shake well with ice and strain into glasses. Serve after dinner.

Sunrise
¼ Cointreau
¼ Yellow Chartreuse
¼ Crème de Violette
¼ Grenadine
Pour carefully into liqueur glass so that ingredients do not mix. Serve after dinner.

CRÈME DE CACAO

Angel's Kiss
¼ Crème de Cacao
¼ Prunelle
¼ Crème de Violette
¼ Sweet Cream
Pour ingredients carefully into glass so that they do not mix.

Angel's Tip
¾ Crème de Cacao
¼ Cream
Pour carefully into liqueur glass, floating Cream on top.

Angel's Wing
½ Crème de Cacao
½ Prunelle
Pour ingredients carefully into glass so that they do not mix and float Cream on top.

Golden Gopher
1 Jigger White Crème de Cacao
1 Jigger Brandy
Stir well with ice and strain into glass.

Layer Cake
⅓ Crème de Cacao
⅓ Apricot Brandy
⅓ Cream
Pour carefully into liqueur glass so that ingredients do not mix. Place Cherry on top. Chill mixture in glass.

Liebfraumilch
1 Jigger Crème de Cacao
1 Jigger Cream
Juice of 1 Lime
Shake well with ice and strain into glass.

Witching Eve
⅔ Crème de Cacao
1 Dash Angostura Bitters
⅓ Cream
Pour carefully into liqueur glass so that ingredients do not mix.

CRÈME DE MENTHE

Diana
¾ White Crème de Menthe
Shaved Ice
¼ Brandy

Place ice in glass and pour in
Crème de Menthe. Top carefully
with Brandy.

Frappé (Crème de Menthe)
Fill cocktail glass with shaved ice.
Pour in Green or White Crème
de Menthe.

Grasshopper
⅔ Jigger Green Crème de
Menthe
⅔ Jigger White Crème de Cacao
⅔ Jigger Cream
Shake well with ice and serve in
Champagne glass.

Pousse Café
⅙ Grenadine
⅙ Maraschino
⅙ Green Crème de Menthe
⅙ Crème de Violette
⅙ Chartreuse
⅙ Brandy
Add carefully in order given to
keep each liqueur separate.

Stinger (see Brandy)

CRÈME DE VIOLETTE

Angel's Wings
⅓ Crème de Violette
⅓ Raspberry Syrup
⅓ Maraschino
Pour ingredients carefully into
liqueur glass so that they do not
mix.

CRÈME D'YVETTE

Lillian Waldorf
½ Jigger Crème d'Yvette
½ Jigger Maraschino
Pour carefully and top with
Cream.

CURAÇAO

Baby's Own
⅔ White Curaçao
⅓ Cream
1 Dash Angostura Bitters
Shake well with ice and strain
into glass.

Canadian No. 1
1 Jigger Curaçao
3 Dashes Jamaica Rum
1 Teaspoon Powdered Sugar
Juice of ½ Lemon
Shake well with ice and strain
into glass.

Curaçao (for 6)
5 Jiggers Curaçao
5 Jiggers Orange Juice
1 Jigger Brandy
1 Jigger Dry Gin
Shake well with ice and strain
into glasses rinsed with Orange
Bitters.

Double Arrow
½ Light Curaçao
½ Crème d'Yvette
Cream
Pour carefully into liqueur glasses
so that liqueurs do not mix, and
top with Cream.

Five Fifteen
1/3 Curaçao
1/3 Dry Vermouth
1/3 Cream
Shake well with ice and strain
into glass.

GRAND MARNIER

Alfonso Special
1/2 Grand Marnier
1/4 Dry Vermouth
1/4 Dry Gin
4 Dashes Sweet Vermouth
1 Dash Angostura Bitters
Stir well with ice and strain into
glass.

Gloom Chaser
1/4 Grand Marnier
1/4 Curaçao
1/4 Lemon Juice
1/4 Grenadine
Stir well with ice and strain into
glass.

Red Lion
2/3 Jigger Grand Marnier
2/3 Jigger Dry Gin
1/3 Jigger Lemon Juice
1/3 Jigger Orange Juice
Shake well with ice and strain
into glass. Serve with twist of
Lemon Peel.

KIRSCH

Café Kirsch
1 Jigger Kirsch
1 Teaspoon Sugar
2 Jiggers Cold Coffee
1 Egg White

Shake well with ice and strain
into glass.

Rose No. 3
1/2 Kirsch
1/2 Dry Vermouth
1 Teaspoon Grenadine
Stir well with ice and strain into
glass.

MARASCHINO

Knickerbein
1 Jigger Maraschino
1 Jigger Grenadine
1 Egg Yolk
1 Jigger Brandy
Shake well with ice and strain
into glass.

SLOE GIN

Sloe Gin No. 1
1 1/2 Jiggers Sloe Gin
1/2 Jigger Dry Vermouth
Stir well with ice and strain into
glass.

Sloe Gin No. 2
1 1/2 Jiggers Sloe Gin
2 Dashes Orange Bitters
2 Dashes Angostura Bitters
Shake well with ice and strain
into glass.

Ninety Miles
1/2 Sloe Gin
1/2 Applejack
Shake well with ice and strain
into glass.

Queen Bee
2/3 Sloe Gin
1/3 Curaçao
1 Dash Anisette
Shake well with ice and strain
into glass.

White Man's Burden
1 Jigger Sloe Gin
1/3 Jigger Apricot Brandy
Juice of 1/2 Lime
Shake well with ice and strain
into glass.

SOUTHERN COMFORT

Memphis Belle
Place 1/2 Peach and a Maraschino
Cherry in a Champagne glass.
Add shaved ice and fill with
Southern Comfort. Serve with
short straws and a small spoon.

Old-Fashioned
Put 1 dash Angostura Bitters in
Old-Fashioned glass. Add a twist
of Lemon Peel and ice cubes. Fill
with Southern Comfort as
desired.

Rhett Butler
1 Jigger Southern Comfort
Juice of 1/4 Lime
Juice of 1/4 Lemon
1 Teaspoon Curaçao
1/2 Teaspoon Powdered Sugar
Shake well with ice and strain
into glass.

Scarlett O'Hara
1 1/2 Jiggers Southern Comfort
1 1/2 Jiggers Cranberry Juice
Juice of 1/4 Lime
Stir well with ice and strain into
glass.

COCKTAILS AND DRINKS—
NON-ALCOHOLIC

Basic Tea Punch
2 Cups Strong Hot Tea
6 Cups Fruit Juice
1/4 Ginger Ale or Soda Water
Combine just before serving and
sweeten to taste with Sugar or
Syrup, etc. Pour over a block of
ice in a punch bowl and chill.

Black Cow
Fill a tall glass 3/4 full of
Sarsaparilla and add 1 or 2
scoops of Vanilla Ice Cream.

Black and Tan
Fill a tall glass, with 1 or 2 ice
cubes, 2/3 full of Cola. Fill up
with Milk. Stir and serve.

Clam Juice Cocktail
Combine in a shaker 1 teaspoon
Tomato Catsup, 1 pinch Celery
Salt, 1 or 2 dashes Tabasco Sauce
and 2/3 cup Clam Juice. Shake
well with 1 or 2 ice cubes and
strain into small tumbler.

Clam Juice-Tomato Cocktail

Prepare same as CLAM JUICE COCKTAIL, omitting Catsup and using half and half Clam Juice and Tomato Juice.

Club Cocktail

1 Lump Sugar
2 Dashes Angostura Bitters
1 Long Twist Lemon Peel
Soda Water
Place Sugar in Old-Fashioned glass and splash with Bitters. Add other ingredients with ice cubes and fill with Soda Water.

Eggnog

1 Egg
1 Teaspoon Sugar
1 Pinch Salt
¼ Teaspoon Vanilla
Milk
Beat Egg with Salt and Sugar. Pour into tall glass, add Vanilla and fill with Milk. Stir and sprinkle lightly with Nutmeg.

Grape Juice Cup (for 10)

Place ice cubes in a large pitcher and add the Juice of 6 Lemons, 1 quart of Grape Juice and fill with Soda Water. Add Grenadine to taste and decorate with fruit as desired. Stir and serve.

Horse's Neck

Rind of 1 Entire Lemon
Ginger Ale
Place in highball glass with ice. Fill with Ginger Ale. (The alcoholic version adds a jigger of American Whiskey.)

Lemonade (for 4 to 6)

Juice of 6 Lemons
1 Quart Water
1 Cup Sugar Syrup or other Sweetening
Combine in pitcher and chill. Pour over ice cubes in tall glasses. Garnish with fruit or Mint as desired.

Orangeade (for 4 to 6)

Juice of 5 Oranges
Juice of 1 Lemon
½ Cup Sugar Syrup
1 Quart Water
Prepare and serve same as LEMONADE.

Parisette

Place in a tumbler several ice cubes, 1 tablespoon Grenadine and fill with cold Milk. Stir and serve.

Pink Pearl (for 6)

1 Cup Grapefruit Juice
2 Teaspoons Lemon Juice
1 or 2 Tablespoons Grenadine
1 or 2 Egg Whites
Shake with crushed ice and strain into cocktail glasses.

Prairie Oyster No. 2

1 Egg Yolk
2 Dashes Vinegar
1 Teaspoon Worcestershire Sauce
1 Dash Tabasco Sauce
1 Pinch Salt
Slip Egg Yolk carefully into small glass. Add seasoning.

Rail Splitter

Juice of ½ Lemon
⅔ Jigger Sugar Syrup
Pour into glass with ice and fill
up with Ginger Beer.

Rosey Squash

Place in a tumbler with ice cubes
the Juice of ½ Lemon, 1
tablespoon Grenadine and fill
up with Soda Water.

Saratoga No. 2

Juice of ½ Lemon
½ Teaspoon Powdered Sugar
2 Dashes Angostura Bitters
Ginger Ale
Place ingredients in tall glass
with ice cubes and fill with
Ginger Ale.

Sherbet Punch (for 12)

Place a large piece of ice in a
punch bowl and add 1 pint
Orange Sherbet and 1 quart
Ginger Ale. Break the Sherbet
into chunks and pour the Ginger
Ale over it. Decorate with Mint
Leaves and serve in punch cups.

Spiced Cider (for 4)

1 Quart Apple Cider
¼ Cup Sugar
⅛ Teaspoon Salt
1 Cinnamon Stick, broken
12 Whole Cloves
8 Whole Allspice
Combine ingredients in a
saucepan and bring to a boil.
Cool and let stand for several
hours. Strain and reheat before
serving.

Spiced Lemonade

1 Cup Sugar Syrup
12 Whole Cloves
1 Stick Cinnamon
Juice of 6 Lemons
1 Quart Water
Cook Sugar, Cloves and
Cinnamon for 5 minutes. Add
Lemon Juice and let stand 1
hour. Add Water and strain into
glasses over crushed ice.

Summer Delight

Place 2 or 3 ice cubes in a large
tumbler. Add the Juice of 1 Lime
and ½ Jigger Raspberry Syrup.
Fill up with Soda Water and
decorate with fruit as desired.
Stir and serve.

Summer Fizz (for 8)

12 Sprigs Mint
½ Cup Lemon Juice
1 Cup Currant Jelly
1 Cup Hot Water
1 Cup Cold Water
3 Cups Orange Juice
1 Bottle Ginger Ale
Crush Mint in a bowl and add
boiling Water and 1 cup Currant
Jelly. When Jelly is melted, add
cold Water. Strain when cold
into punch bowl. Add Fruit
Juices and block of ice. Just
before serving, pour in Ginger
Ale and decorate with Mint.

Temperance Cup (for 10)

Combine in punch bowl, with a
block of ice, the Juice of 4
Oranges, the Juice of 1 Lemon,
the Juice of 5 Limes, 3

tablespoons Powdered Sugar and 1 quart Grape Juice. Stir and decorate with fruit as desired.

Temperance Punch
½ Pound Powdered Sugar
1 Quart Cold Tea
1 Pint Lemon Juice
1 Quart Soda Water
2 Quarts White Grape Juice
Combine all ingredients in punch bowl with a block of ice. Stir and decorate with fruit as desired.

Tomato Juice Cocktail
Combine in shaker with ice ⅔ cup Tomato Juice, Juice of ¼ Lemon, 1 pinch of Salt, 1 teaspoon Worcestershire Sauce. Shake well and strain into small tumbler.

Virgin Mary
Same as TOMATO JUICE COCKTAIL with a dash of Tabasco. Serve in large glass over ice.

COCKTAILS—RUM BASE

Apple Pie
½ Light Rum
½ Sweet Vermouth
4 Dashes Apricot Brandy
4 Dashes Lemon Juice
2 Dashes Grenadine
Shake well with ice and strain
into glass.

Bacardi No. 1
2 Jiggers Bacardi Rum
Juice of ½ Lime
2 Dashes Sugar Syrup
Shake well with ice and strain
into glass.

Bacardi No. 2
Prepare same as No. 1,
substituting Grenadine for Sugar
Syrup.

Bacardi Special
⅔ Bacardi Rum
⅓ English Gin
Juice of ½ Lime
1 Teaspoon Grenadine

Shake well with ice and strain
into glass.

Bahia
1 Jigger Light Rum
1 Jigger Medium Rum
1 Jigger Coconut Cream
(Canned)
2 Jiggers Pineapple Juice,
Unsweetened
Shake hard with cracked ice or
stir in blender.

Beachcomber
1½ Jiggers Light Rum
½ Jigger Cointreau
Juice of ½ Lime
2 Dashes Maraschino
Shake with shaved ice and serve
in large cocktail glass.

Bee's Kiss
1 Jigger Rum
1 Teaspoon Honey
1 Teaspoon Cream
Shake well with ice and strain
into glass.

Bolo
2 Jiggers Light Rum
Juice of ½ Lemon or Lime
Juice of ¼ Orange
1 Teaspoon Powdered Sugar
Shake well with ice and strain
into glass.

Bushranger
½ Light Rum
½ Dubonnet
2 Dashes Angostura Bitters
Shake well with ice and strain
into glass.

Chinese
⅔ Dark Rum
⅓ Grenadine
3 Dashes Curaçao
3 Dashes Maraschino
1 Dash Angostura Bitters
Stir well with ice and strain into
glass. Serve with Cherry.

Clayton's Special
½ Light Rum
¼ Cola
¼ Sirop de Citron
Shake well with ice and strain
into glass.

Columbia
1 Jigger Light Rum
⅓ Jigger Raspberry Syrup
⅓ Lemon Juice
Shake well with ice and strain
into glass.

Country Life
½ Jigger Dark Rum
½ Jigger Port
1 Jigger Bourbon Whiskey
3 Dashes Angostura Bitters
1 Dash Orange Bitters

Shake well with ice and strain
into glass.

Cuba Libre
2 Jiggers Medium Rum
Juice of 1 Lime
Fill large glass with ice. Fill with
Cola.

Cuban No. 2 (see Bacardi No. 1)

Cuban No. 3
1½ Jiggers Light Rum
½ Jigger Apricot Brandy
Juice of ½ Lime
Shake well with ice and strain
into glass.

Cuban No. 4
1 Jigger Light Rum
1 Jigger Pineapple Juice
1 Teaspoon Grenadine
1 Teaspoon Maraschino
Fill large glass with shaved ice
and pour mixed ingredients over.
Serve with straws.

Daiquiri
1½ Jiggers Light Rum
Juice of ½ Lime
1 Teaspoon Powdered Sugar
Shake well with ice and strain
into glass.

Daiquiri (frozen)
2 Jiggers Light Rum
1 Tablespoon Lime or Lemon
Juice
2 Teaspoons Powdered Sugar
Place 2 cups shaved ice in a
blender. Add ingredients and
blend until consistency of snow.
Serve immediately with straw.

With a blender, fresh or frozen fruit or juices may be added to the DAIQUIRI, as desired. Sometimes a dash of Maraschino and/or Grenadine is added.

Daiquiri (banana)
Same as DAIQUIRI (frozen) with an inch of Banana added.

Davis
½ Dark Rum
½ Dry Vermouth
2 Dashes Raspberry Syrup
Juice of 1 Lime
Shake well with ice and strain into glass.

Dunlop
⅔ Light Rum
⅓ Sherry
1 Dash Angostura Bitters
Stir well with ice and strain into glass.

El Presidente
1 Jigger Light Rum
⅓ Jigger Curaçao
⅓ Jigger Dry Vermouth
1 Dash Grenadine
Shake well with ice and strain into glass.

Eyeopener
1 Jigger Light Rum
2 Dashes Crème de Noyau
2 Dashes Curaçao
2 Dashes Pernod
1 Teaspoon Powdered Sugar
1 Egg Yolk
Shake well with ice and strain into glass.

Fair and Warmer
⅔ Light Rum
⅓ Sweet Vermouth
2 Dashes Curaçao
Stir well with ice and strain into glass. Serve with twist of Lemon Peel.

Fireman's Sour
2 Jiggers Light Rum
½ Teaspoon Powdered Sugar
Juice of 1 Lime
⅓ Jigger Grenadine
Shake well with ice and strain into Delmonico glass. Decorate with fruit if desired.

Flanagan
1 Jigger Dark Rum
1 Jigger Sweet Vermouth
½ Teaspoon Sugar Syrup
1 Dash Angostura Bitters
Shake well with ice and strain into glass.

Florida Special No. 1
1 Jigger Light Rum
1 Teaspoon Dry Vermouth
1 Teaspoon Sweet Vermouth
⅔ Jigger Unsweetened Grapefruit Juice
Stir with shaved ice and strain into glass.

Fluffy Ruffles
½ Light Rum
½ Sweet Vermouth
1 Twist of Lime or Lemon Peel
Stir well with ice and strain into glass.

Fog Cutter
2 Jiggers Medium Rum
1 Jigger Brandy
½ Jigger Dry Gin
2 Jiggers Lemon Juice
1 Jigger Orange Juice
½ Jigger Orgeat Syrup
Sherry
Shake all but Sherry with cracked ice. Pour into large glass. Float Sherry.

Four Flush
½ Light Rum
¼ Swedish Punch
¼ Dry Vermouth
1 Dash Grenadine or Sugar Syrup
Stir well with ice and strain into glass.

Fox Trot
2 Jiggers Light Rum
2 Dashes Curaçao
Juice of ½ Lime or Lemon
Shake well with ice and strain into glass.

Governor's
Before your cocktail party place 1 Vanilla Bean in a bottle of Light Rum and leave it 24 hours. For your drinks place 1 or 2 ice cubes in a Champagne glass with 1 teaspoon Sugar Syrup and 1 twist Lime Peel. Fill up with Rum.

Gradeal Special
½ Light Rum
¼ Apricot Brandy
¼ Dry Gin
Stir well with ice and strain into glass.

Havana Club
1 Jigger Medium Rum
½ Jigger Dry Vermouth
Stir well with ice and strain into glass.

Hawaiian
1 Jigger Dark Rum
1 Jigger Pineapple Juice, Unsweetened
1 Egg White
Dash Orange Bitters
Shake well with ice and strain into glass.

Honeybee
1½ Jiggers Light Rum
⅓ Jigger Lemon Juice
1 Tablespoon Honey
Shake well with ice and strain into glass.

Honeysuckle
1 Jigger Medium Rum
1 Teaspoon Honey
Juice of ½ Lime or Lemon
Shake very well with ice and strain into glass.

Irish Elegance
⅘ Jigger Dark Rum
⅕ Jigger Brandy
1 Teaspoon Crème de Violette
⅓ Jigger Pineapple Juice
½ Teaspoon Sugar
Juice of 1 Lime
Mix in blender with shaved ice and serve immediately.

Jamaica Ginger
⅔ Dark Rum
⅓ Grenadine
3 Dashes Maraschino
3 Dashes Curaçao
1 Dash Angostura Bitters
Shake well with ice and strain into glass.

Joburg
1 Jigger Light Rum
1 Jigger Dubonnet
4 Dashes Orange Bitters
Stir well with ice and strain into glass. Serve with twist of Lemon Peel.

Kicker
⅔ Light Rum
⅓ Calvados or Apple Brandy
2 Dashes Sweet Vermouth
Stir well with ice and strain into glass.

Kingston No. 1
½ Dark Rum
¼ Kümmel
¼ Orange Juice
1 Dash Pimento Dram
Shake well with ice and strain into glass.

Kingston No. 2
1 Jigger Dark Rum
½ Jigger Gin
Juice of ½ Lime or Lemon
1 Teaspoon Grenadine
Shake well with ice and strain into glass.

Knickerbocker Special
⅔ Medium Rum
⅓ Curaçao
1 Slice Pineapple, crushed
1 Teaspoon Orange Juice
1 Teaspoon Lemon Juice
1 Teaspoon Raspberry Syrup
Shake well with ice and strain into glass.

La Florida
1⅓ Jiggers Light Rum
1 Teaspoon Sugar
1 Teaspoon Maraschino
Juice of ½ Lemon
Shaved Ice
Shake well and serve frappé, with a small straw.

Leilani
2 Jiggers Hawaiian Rum
½ Jigger Each Lemon, Pineapple, and Dash Papaya Juice
Dash Grenadine
Pour into large glass with ice. Fill with Club Soda.

Little Princess
½ Light Rum
½ Sweet Vermouth
Stir well with ice and strain into glass.

Mai Tai
There are several interpretations and now a number of "mixes."
1 Jigger Dark or Medium Rum
Juice of 1 Lime
½ Jigger Curaçao
Dash Sugar Syrup
Dollop Orgeat
Shake hard with ice and pour into large glass.

Maragato (Special)

⅓ Light Rum
⅓ Dry Vermouth
⅓ Sweet Vermouth
1 Dash Kirsch
Juice of ½ Lemon
Juice of ⅓ Lime
½ Teaspoon Sugar, dissolved in water
Shake well with ice and strain into glass.

Marvel

¾ Dark Rum
⅛ Grenadine
⅛ Sirop de Citron
Shake well with ice and strain into glass.

Mary Pickford

½ Light Rum
½ Pineapple Juice
1 Teaspoon Grenadine
1 Dash Maraschino
Stir well with ice and strain into glass.

Melba

½ Jigger Light Rum
2 Dashes Pernod
½ Jigger Swedish Punch
Juice of ½ Lime
2 Dashes Grenadine
Shake well with ice and strain into glass.

Miami

1 Jigger Light Rum
½ Jigger White Crème de Menthe
2 or 3 Dashes Lemon Juice
Shake well with ice and strain into glass.

Miami Beach

1 Jigger Light Rum
½ Jigger Cointreau
1 Dash Lemon or Lime Juice
Shake well with ice and strain into glass.

Million

⅔ Dark Rum
⅓ Lime Juice
½ Teaspoon Powdered Sugar
1 Dash Angostura Bitters
Shake well with shaved ice and strain into glass. Serve with a Cherry.

Millionaire No. 2

⅓ Dark Rum
⅓ Apricot Brandy
⅓ Sloe Gin
1 Dash Grenadine
Juice of 1 Lime
Shake well with ice and strain into glass.

Morning Rose

½ Jigger Light Rum
½ Jigger Curaçao
⅓ Jigger Grenadine
⅓ Jigger Lemon Juice
Shake well with ice and strain into glass.

Naked Lady

½ Light Rum
½ Sweet Vermouth
4 Dashes Apricot Brandy
2 Dashes Grenadine
4 Dashes Lemon Juice
Shake well with ice and strain into glass.

National
1⅓ Jiggers Light Rum
⅓ Jigger Pineapple Juice
⅓ Jigger Apricot Brandy
Shake well with shaved ice and
strain into glass. Serve with
Pineapple (stick or wedge) and
Cherry.

Nevada
1½ Jiggers Light Rum
Juice of ½ Grapefruit
Juice of 1 Lime
1 Dash Angostura Bitters
1 Teaspoon Powdered Sugar
Shake well with ice and strain
into glass.

Olympia
1 Jigger Dark Rum
⅔ Jigger Cherry Brandy
Juice of ½ Lime
Shake well with ice and strain
into glass.

Palmetto
½ Medium Rum
½ Sweet Vermouth
2 Dashes Orange Bitters
Stir well with ice and strain into
glass. Serve with twist of Lemon
Peel.

Panama
1 Jigger Dark Rum
½ Jigger Crème de Cacao
½ Jigger Cream
Shake well with ice and strain
into glass.

Paradise
1½ Jiggers Light Rum
½ Jigger Apricot Brandy

Shake well with ice and strain
into glass.

Parisian Blonde
⅓ Dark Rum
⅓ Curaçao
⅓ Cream
Shake well with ice and strain
into glass.

Passion (for 4)
1 Jigger Dark Rum
4 Jiggers Light Rum
1 Teaspoon Honey
Juice of 2 Limes
Shake well with ice and strain
into glasses.

Pauline
½ Light Rum
½ Sweetened Lemon Juice
1 Dash Pernod
1 Grating of Nutmeg
Shake well with ice and strain
into glass.

Pilgrim
1 Jigger New England Rum
1 Teaspoon Grenadine
Juice of ½ Lime or Lemon
Shake well with ice and strain
into glass.

Pirate's
2 Parts Dark Rum
1 Sweet Vermouth
1 Dash Angostura Bitters
Stir well with ice and strain into
glass.

Planter's No. 1
½ Dark Rum
½ Orange Juice
1 Dash Lemon Juice

Shake well with ice and strain into glass.

Planter's No. 2
½ Dark Rum
¼ Lemon Juice
¼ Sugar Syrup
Stir well with ice and strain into glass.

Planter's Punch
3 Parts Jamaica Rum
1 Part Lime Juice
2 Parts Sugar Syrup
3 Parts Water (including ice) or Soda
A Dash of Curaçao or of Angostura can do no harm (optional). Use a tall glass. Garnish with cherries and orange slices.
Note: There is no *one* way to make this drink. Every Caribbean island makes it, and usually of its own native rum.

Platinum Blonde
1 Part Light Rum
1 Cointreau
⅓ Jigger Cream
Shake well with ice and strain into glass.

Poker (see Little Princess)

President
1 Jigger Light Rum
Juice of ¼ Orange
2 Dashes Grenadine
Shake well with ice and strain into glass.

Quarter Deck No. 1
⅔ Dark Rum
⅓ Sherry
1 Teaspoon Lime Juice
Stir well with ice and strain into glass.

Quarter Deck No. 2
½ Dark Rum
¼ Dry Sherry
¼ Scotch Whisky
1 Teaspoon Sugar Syrup
1 Dash Orange Bitters
Shake well with ice and strain into glass.

Robson
½ Dark Rum
¼ Grenadine
⅛ Orange Juice
⅛ Lemon Juice
Shake well with ice and strain into glass.

Royal Bermuda
2 Ounces Medium Rum
Juice of 1 Lime
Little Sugar Syrup
1 Dash Cointreau
Shake with shaved ice and strain into glass.

Rum Collins
1 Jigger Light Rum
⅔ Jigger Lemon Juice
⅓ Jigger Sugar Syrup
Pour into large glass with ice. Fill with Soda.

Rum Dubonnet
½ Jigger Light Rum
½ Jigger Dubonnet
Juice of ½ Lime

Stir well with ice and strain into glass.

Rum Frappé
Place 1 scoop Orange or Lemon Sherbet in a Champagne glass and cover with Rum as desired. Stir and serve.

Rum Gimlet
4 Parts Medium Rum
1 Part Rose's Lime Juice
Mix well over ice.

Rum Havana
1 Jigger Light Rum
2/3 Jigger Pineapple Juice
1/4 Jigger Lemon Juice
Shake well with ice and strain into glass.

Rummy
1 Ounce Dark Rum
1 Ounce Dry Vermouth
1/2 Ounce Lime Juice
1/2 Ounce Grenadine
Shake well with ice and strain into glass.

Rum Old-Fashioned
Place 1 small lump Sugar in Old-Fashioned glass and sprinkle with a few drops of Angostura or Orange Bitters. Add 1 large twist Lemon Peel and fill glass with ice cubes. Pour in Medium Rum as desired and muddle. A slice of Lemon or Orange or a Cherry may be added.

Rum-on-the-Rocks
Fill Old-Fashioned glass with cracked ice. Pour Rum in as desired. Serve with Lemon Peel.

Rum Screwdriver
1 Jigger Medium Rum
2 Jiggers Orange Juice
Serve with plenty of ice.

Rum Sour
2 Jiggers Dark Rum
Juice of 1 Lime
Sugar Syrup to taste
Shake well with shaved ice and strain into Delmonico glass. Add slice of Orange and Cherry if desired.

Rum/Tonic
Rum mixes quite well with Tonic, Fresca, Squirt or any of the others.

Santiago
2 Jiggers Bacardi Rum
2 Dashes Grenadine
4 Dashes Lime Juice
Stir well with ice and strain into glass.

Saxon
1 Jigger Light Rum
2 Dashes Grenadine
1 Twist Orange Peel
Juice of 1/2 Lime
Shake well with ice and strain into glass.

Scorpion
2 Jiggers Light Rum
1 Jigger Brandy
1 1/2 Jiggers Lemon Juice
2 Jiggers Orange Juice
1/2 Jigger Orgeat
Use blender and plenty of ice.

September Morn
2 Jiggers Light Rum
3 Dashes Grenadine
Juice of ½ Lime
1 Egg White
Shake well with ice and strain
into glass.

Sevilla No. 1
½ Dark Rum
½ Sweet Vermouth
1 Twist Orange Peel
Stir well with ice and strain into
glass.

Sevilla No. 2
½ Light Rum
½ Port
1 Egg
½ Teaspoon Powdered Sugar
Shake well with ice and strain
into glass.

Shanghai
1 Jigger Dark Rum
⅔ Ounce Lemon Juice
⅓ Ounce Anisette
2 Dashes Grenadine
Stir well with ice and strain into
glass.

Shark's Tooth
1 Jigger Light Rum
½ Jigger 151 Proof Rum
½ Jigger Lemon Juice
½ Jigger Lime Juice
Dash Sugar Syrup
Dash Grenadine
Pour into large glass with ice.
Top with Soda.

Sonora
½ Light Rum
½ Calvados or Applejack
2 Dashes Apricot Brandy
1 Dash Lemon Juice
Stir well with ice and strain into
glass.

Spanish Town
1 Jigger Medium Rum
2 Dashes Curaçao
Shake with shaved ice and strain
into glass. Serve with a grating
of Nutmeg.

Suffering Bastard
2 Jiggers Dark Rum
1 Jigger Light Rum
Juice of 1 Lime
½ Jigger Mai Tai mix (or make
your own—½ Curaçao,
½ Orgeat)
Garnish with strip Cucumber
Rind.

Sunshine No. 2
½ Light Rum
½ Dry Vermouth
2 Dashes Crème de Cassis
Juice of 1 Lime
Stir well with ice and strain into
glass.

Surprised
2 Jiggers Jamaica Rum
1 Jigger Kümmel
1 Jigger Orange Juice
1 Dash Pimento Dram
Shake well with shaved ice and
strain into glasses.

Swing

⅓ Light Rum
⅓ Cointreau
⅓ Dry Gin
1 Dash Pernod
Shake well with shaved ice and strain into glass.

Tanglefoot

⅓ Light Rum
⅓ Swedish Punch
⅙ Orange Juice
⅙ Lemon Juice
Shake well with ice and strain into glass.

Trinidad

1½ Jiggers Dark Rum
Juice of ½ Lime
1 Teaspoon Powdered Sugar
3 Dashes Angostura Bitters
Shake well with ice and strain into glass.

Wedding March

2 Jiggers Light Rum
Juice of ½ Lime
2 Egg Whites
2 Dashes Angostura Bitters
Shake well with ice and strain into glass.

Wedding Night

3 Jiggers Medium Rum
½ Jigger Maple Syrup
1 Jigger Lime Juice
Shake with shaved ice and strain into Champagne glass.

West Indies

Add Pineapple Juice to taste to
DAIQUIRI (frozen).

White Lion

1 Jigger Dark Rum
Juice of ½ Lemon
1 Teaspoon Powdered Sugar
3 Dashes Angostura Bitters
3 Dashes Raspberry Syrup
Shake well with ice and strain into glass.

X.Y.Z.

½ Dark Rum
¼ Cointreau
¼ Lemon Juice
Shake well with ice and strain into glass.

Yo Ho

⅓ Medium Rum
⅓ Swedish Punch
⅓ Calvados or Apple Brandy
Shake well with ice and strain into glass. Serve with twist of Lemon Peel.

Zombie

1 Jigger Dark Rum
1 Jigger Medium Rum
1 Jigger Light Rum
1 Jigger Pineapple Juice
1 Jigger Papaya Juice (optional)
Juice of 1 Lime
1 Teaspoon Powdered Sugar
Shake well with ice. Pour into tall glass. Garnish with Pineapple and Cherries. On top float a little Medium Rum.

COCKTAILS—TEQUILA BASE

Acapulco
1 Jigger Tequila
1 Jigger Jamaica Rum
2 Jiggers Pineapple Juice
½ Jigger Grapefruit Juice
Shake well with ice cubes.

Bertha
1 Jigger Tequila
Juice of ½ Lime
Dash Grenadine
Shake with ice cubes. Pour into
glass and fill with Grapefruit
Juice.

Bloody Bull
1 Jigger Tequila
½ Jigger Lemon Juice
Dash Worcestershire and
Tabasco
Mix over ice in large glass. Fill
with Bouillon and Tomato Juice,
half and half.

El Diablo
1 Jigger Tequila
Juice of ½ Lime
½ Jigger Crème de Cassis
Stir with ice in large glass. Fill
with Ginger Ale.

Margarita (or Grande)
1 Jigger Tequila
½ Jigger Triple Sec or Cointreau
Juice of ½ Lime
Stir over ice.

Mexican Lover
1 Jigger Tequila
½ Jigger Brandy
½ Jigger Sweet Vermouth
Stir well over ice.

Picador
2 Parts Tequila
1 Part Kahlua or Tia Maria
Stir well with ice.

Prado
1 Jigger Tequila
Juice of ½ Lemon
A Little Egg White
Dollop Maraschino
Dash Grenadine
Shake vigorously with ice.

Sangrita
1 Jigger Tequila
2 Jiggers Sangrita Mix
Stir well with ice.

Tequila España
1 Part Tequila
1 Part Medium Sherry
Chill with ice. Serve in wine
glass.

Tequila Matador
1 Jigger Tequila
2 Jiggers Unsweetened
Pineapple Juice
Juice of ½ Lime
Chill well with ice.

Tequila Neat (The original way of drinking tequila)
Wedge of Lemon
Pinch of Salt
1 Jigger Tequila
Put Salt in notch of thumb and forefinger of left hand. Hold Lemon in left hand. In right hand, hold small glass with Tequila. Now suck Lemon, take a lick of Salt, swallow Tequila.

Tequila Sunrise
1 Jigger Tequila
⅓ Teaspoon Crème de Cassis
1 Teaspoon Grenadine
Juice of ½ Lime
Stir everything with ice in tall glass. Fill with Soda.

COCKTAILS—VODKA BASE

Barbara or Russian Bear
½ Vodka
¼ Crème de Cacao
¼ Cream
Stir well with ice and strain into glass.

Black Russian
1 Jigger Vodka
½ Jigger Kahlua
Shake or stir with ice (with Tia Maria the drink is sometimes called a Black Cloud).

Bloody Mary
1 Jigger Vodka
2 Jiggers Tomato Juice
⅓ Jigger Lemon Juice
1 Dash Worcestershire Sauce
Salt and Pepper to taste
Shake well with ice and strain into glass.

Blue Monday or Caucasian
¾ Vodka
¼ Contreau
1 Dash Blue Vegetable Extract (coloring)

Stir well with ice and strain into glass. Coloring may be omitted.

Bullshot
1 Jigger Vodka
1 Teaspoon Lemon Juice
Dollop Worcestershire Sauce
Dash Tabasco Sauce
Mix in large glass. Add ice. Fill with chilled Beef Bouillon
(For a "Bloody Bullshot," use Tomato Juice, half and half with Bouillon.)

Cape Codder
1 Jigger Vodka
2 Jiggers Cranberry Juice
Juice of ½ Lime or ¼ Lemon
Stir over ice cubes. (Use Cranberry Cordial in place of Cranberry Juice—voilà, the Red Russian.)

Clam and Tomato
1 Jigger Vodka
2 Jiggers Clam Juice
2 Jiggers Tomato Juice
Dash Tabasco
Stir over ice cubes.

The Gazebo
1 Jigger Vodka
½ Jigger Apricot Brandy
2 Jiggers Pineapple Juice
2 Dashes Grenadine
Shake with ice. Serve in
Champagne flute.

Gimlet (with Vodka—usually made with Gin)
1 Jigger Vodka
1 Jigger Rose's Unsweetened
Lime Juice
Stir with cracked ice.

Godmother
1 Jigger Vodka
1 Jigger Amaretto
Stir with cracked ice.

Golden Screw or Golden Spike
1 Jigger Vodka
3 Jiggers Orange Juice
Shake with ice and strain into
glass or serve in tall glass with
ice cubes.

Harvey Wallbanger
1 Jigger Vodka
3 Jiggers Orange Juice
½ Jigger Galliano
In tall glass filled with ice cubes,
put Vodka, fill with Orange
Juice, float Galliano atop.

Kangaroo
1 Jigger Vodka
½ Jigger Dry Vermouth
Stir with cracked ice and strain
into glass. Serve with twist of
Lemon Peel.

Moscow Mule
1 Jigger Vodka
Juice of 1 Lime
Mix. Pour into mug with ice.
Fill with Ginger Beer.

Russian
1 Jigger Vodka
1 Jigger Dry Gin
1 Jigger Crème de Cacao
Stir well with ice and strain into
glass.

Salty Dog
1 Jigger Vodka
Pour into large glass with ice
cubes. Fill with Unsweetened
Grapefruit Juice.

Screwdriver
1 Jigger Vodka
Pour into large glass with ice
cubes. Fill with Orange Juice.

Sunstroke
1 Jigger Vodka
2 Jiggers Unsweetened
Grapefruit Juice
Dollop Triple Sec or Cointreau
Stir with cracked ice.

Tom Collins (with Vodka—usually made with Gin)
1 Jigger Vodka
⅔ Jigger Lemon Juice
½ Jigger Sugar Syrup
Pour into large glass. Fill with
Soda.

Tovarich
1 Jigger Vodka
⅔ Jigger Kümmel
Juice of ½ Lime

Shake with cracked ice and strain into glass.

Vodka
1 Jigger Vodka
½ Jigger Cherry Brandy
Juice of ½ Lemon or Lime
Shake with ice and strain into glass.

Vodka Gibson
2 Jiggers Vodka
½ Jigger Dry Vermouth
Stir well with ice and strain into glass. Serve with Pickled Pearl Onion.

Vodka Martini
4 or 5 Parts Vodka
1 Part Dry Vermouth
Stir well with ice and strain into glass. Serve with a twist of Lemon Peel.

Vodka-on-the-Rocks
Fill Old-Fashioned glass with ice cubes. Fill with Vodka as desired, and serve with a twist of Lemon Peel.

Vodka/Tonic (or Vodka/7)
1 Jigger Vodka
Pour in large glass with ice. Fill with 7-Up or fill with Tonic Water.

Volcano
⅔ Jigger Vodka
⅓ Jigger Light Rum
1 Jigger Southern Comfort
Shake with cracked ice.

Volga Boatman
1 Jigger Vodka
1 Jigger Cherry Brandy
1 Jigger Orange Juice
Stir well with ice and strain into glass.

COCKTAILS—WHISKEY BASE

Note: Cocktails with Sugar and/or fruit in an Old-Fashioned glass should always be served with a muddler or a small spoon.

Affinity (or Perfect Rob Roy)
⅓ Scotch Whisky
⅓ Dry Vermouth
⅓ Sweet Vermouth
2 Dashes Angostura Bitters
Stir well with ice and strain into glass. Serve with a Cherry and twist of Lemon Peel over top of glass.

Alice
⅓ Scotch Whisky
⅓ Kümmel
⅓ Sweet Vermouth
Stir well with ice and strain into glass.

Appetizer No. 3
2 Jiggers Rye Whiskey
3 Dashes Curaçao
2 Dashes Peychaud's Bitters
1 Twist each Lemon and Orange Peel

Shake well with ice and strain into glass.

Artist's Special
⅓ Whiskey
⅓ Sherry
⅙ Lemon Juice
⅙ Sugar Syrup
Stir well with ice and strain into glass.

Automobile
⅓ Scotch Whisky
⅓ Dry Gin
⅓ Sweet Vermouth
1 Dash Orange Bitters
Stir well with ice and strain into glass.

Barney French
Place 1 slice Orange, 2 dashes Peychaud's Bitters, 1 twist Lemon Peel, 1 or 2 cubes ice in an Old-Fashioned glass and muddle well. Add 1 or 2 jiggers Whiskey and serve.

Blackthorn
½ Irish Whiskey
½ Dry Vermouth
3 Dashes Pernod
3 Dashes Angostura Bitters
Stir well with ice and strain into
glass.

Blinker
1 Jigger Rye or Blended Whiskey
1½ Jiggers Grapefruit Juice
½ Jigger Grenadine
Shake well with ice and strain
into glass.

Blood and Sand
¼ Scotch Whisky
¼ Cherry Brandy
¼ Sweet Vermouth
¼ Orange Juice
Stir well with ice and strain into
glass.

Bobby Burns
Same as AFFINITY, with a dash
of Benedictine added.

Boilermaker
Serve 1 large jigger of Whiskey
straight, with a Beer chaser.

Boomerang
⅓ Rye Whiskey
⅓ Swedish Punch
⅓ Dry Vermouth
1 Dash Angostura Bitters
1 Dash Lemon Juice
Stir well with ice and strain into
glass.

Bourbon Cola
1 Jigger Bourbon
Fill glass with Cola (or other
popular soft drink).

Bourbon Mist
2 Jiggers Bourbon
Fill Old-Fashioned glass with
shaved ice. Pour in Whiskey.

Bourbon Side Car
1 Jigger Bourbon
½ Jigger Triple Sec or Cointreau
Juice of ½ Lime
Shake well with cracked ice.

Bourbon Stinger
1 Jigger Bourbon
⅔ Jigger White Crème de
Menthe
Shake well over cracked ice.

Brainstorm
2 Jiggers Irish Whiskey
2 Dashes Dry Vermouth
2 Dashes Benedictine
1 Twist Orange Peel
Place ingredients in Old-
Fashioned glass with ice cubes.

Broken Leg
1 Jigger Bourbon
3 Jiggers Hot Cider or Apple
Juice
4 or 5 Raisins
Cinnamon Stick or a Shake of
Cinnamon
Lemon Slice
Pour all into serving mug.

Brooklyn
⅔ Rye Whiskey
⅓ Dry Vermouth
1 Dash Maraschino
1 Dash Amer Picon
Stir well with ice and strain into
glass.

Cablegram
2 Jiggers Rye Whiskey
1 Teaspoon Powdered Sugar
Juice of ½ Lemon
Stir well with ice and strain into
large cocktail glass and fill with
dash of Ginger Ale.

Cameron's Kick
⅓ Scotch Whisky
⅓ Irish Whiskey
⅙ Lemon Juice
⅙ Orgeat Syrup
Stir well with ice and strain into
glass.

Canadian No. 2
1 Jigger Canadian Whiskey
1 Dash Curaçao
2 Dashes Angostura Bitters
1 Teaspoon Powdered Sugar
Shake well with ice and strain
into glass.

Capetown
½ Bourbon or Blended Whiskey
½ Dubonnet
3 Dashes Curaçao
1 Dash Angostura Bitters
Stir well with ice and strain into
glass. Serve with twist of Lemon
Peel.

Choker (for 6)
8 Jiggers Whiskey
4 Jiggers Pernod
1 Dash Bitters
Shake very well with shaved ice
and strain into glasses.

Commodore
2 Jiggers Rye Whiskey
Juice of ½ Lime or ¼ Lemon
2 Dashes Orange Bitters
1 Teaspoon Sugar Syrup
Shake well with ice and strain
into glass.

Continental
1 Jigger Scotch
⅔ Jigger Kahlua or Tia Maria
1 Jigger Milk
Stir over ice cubes.

Corn Popper (for 10)
1 Pint Corn Whiskey
1 Cup Cream
2 Egg Whites
1 Tablespoon Grenadine
Shake without ice and fill
cocktail glasses ½ full. Add 1 ice
cube to each and fill with Soda
Water.

Cowboy
⅔ Whiskey
⅓ Cream
Shake with shaved ice and strain
into glass.

Creole
½ Whiskey
½ Sweet Vermouth
2 Dashes Benedictine
2 Dashes Amer Picon
Stir with ice and strain into glass.
Serve with twist of Lemon Peel.

Crow
⅔ Whiskey
⅓ Lemon Juice
1 Dash Grenadine
Stir well with ice and strain into
glass.

Dandy
½ Rye Whiskey
½ Dubonnet
1 Dash Angostura Bitters
3 Dashes Cointreau
1 Twist each Lemon and Orange Peel
Stir well with ice and strain into glass.

Derby No. 2
½ Whiskey
¼ Sweet Vermouth
¼ White Curaçao
Juice of ½ Lime
Shake well with ice and strain into glass. Garnish with a Mint Leaf.

De Rigueur
½ Whiskey
¼ Grapefruit Juice
¼ Honey
Shake well with ice and strain into glass.

Deshler
1 Jigger Rye Whiskey
1 Jigger Dubonnet
2 Dashes Peychaud's Bitters
2 Dashes Cointreau
2 Twists Orange Peel
1 Twist Lemon Peel
Shake well with ice and strain into glass. Serve with a twist of Orange Peel.

Dinah
1 Jigger American Whiskey
1 Jigger Sweetened Lemon Juice
1 Sprig Fresh Mint, slightly bruised
Shake with shaved ice and strain into glasses. Garnish with Mint Leaves.

Dixie (for 6)
6 Jiggers Bourbon Whiskey
2 Teaspoons Sugar
2 Dashes Angostura Bitters
1 Teaspoon Lemon Juice
1 Teaspoon Curaçao
2 Teaspoons White Crème de Menthe
Shake well with ice and strain into glasses. Garnish with Mint Leaves.

Duppy (for 6)
Pour 6 jiggers of Whiskey into a mixing glass and add a few Cloves. Let soak for about 1 hour. Add 5 or 6 drops Orange Bitters and 1 jigger Curaçao. Shake well with ice and strain into glasses.

Earthquake
⅓ Whiskey
⅓ Gin
⅓ Pernod
Shake well with ice and strain into glass.

Edward VIII
Place in an Old-Fashioned glass 2 jiggers Bourbon Whiskey, 1 dash Pernod and 2 teaspoons each Sweet Vermouth and Water. Add 1 or 2 ice cubes and twist of Orange Peel. Stir and serve.

Egg Nog (for 1)
1 Jigger Bourbon
1 Whole Egg
1 Tablespoon Powdered Sugar
1 Glass Milk (or half and half)
Shake hard with ice. Pinch of
Nutmeg goes on top.

Elk's Own
½ Bourbon Whiskey
½ Port
1 Egg White
Juice of ½ Lemon
1 Teaspoon Sugar
Shake well with ice and strain
into glass. Serve with small
wedge of Pineapple (optional).

Evans
2 Jiggers Rye Whiskey
1 Dash Apricot Brandy
1 Dash Curaçao
Stir with ice and strain.

Evening Gun (see Duppy)

Everybody's Irish
1 Jigger Irish Whiskey
6 Dashes Green Chartreuse
3 Dashes Green Crème de
Menthe
Stir well with ice and strain into
glass. Serve with Green Olive.

Everything But
¼ Whiskey
¼ Gin
¼ Lemon Juice
¼ Orange Juice
1 Egg
1 Teaspoon Apricot Brandy
½ Teaspoon Powdered Sugar
Shake well with ice and strain
into glass.

Fans
⅔ Jigger Scotch Whisky
⅓ Jigger Cointreau
⅓ Jigger Unsweetened
Grapefruit Juice
Shake well with ice and strain
into glass.

Flu
2 Jiggers Rye Whiskey
1 Teaspoon Ginger Brandy
1 Teaspoon Rock Candy Syrup
1 Dollop Jamaica Rum
Juice of ¼ Lemon
Stir well without ice and strain
into glass. This is supposedly a
medicine.

Flying Scot (for 6)
6 Jiggers Scotch Whisky
4 Jiggers Sweet Vermouth
1 Tablespoon Sugar Syrup
1 Tablespoon Bitters
Shake well with ice and strain
into glasses.

Frisco
1 Jigger Bourbon Whiskey
½ Jigger Benedictine
Stir with shaved ice and strain
into glass. Serve with twist of
Lemon Peel.

Godfather
1 Jigger Scotch or Bourbon
⅔ Jigger Amaretto
Stir over ice cubes.

Grace's Delight (for 6)
4 Jiggers Bourbon or Blended Whiskey
5 Jiggers Dry Vermouth
1 Jigger Framboise
Juice of ½ Orange
1 Teaspoon Orange Bitters
1 Teaspoon Orange Flower Water
1 Pinch Cinnamon
1 Pinch Nutmeg
3 Juniper Berries
Combine all ingredients in shaker and place on ice for 1 hour. Shake without ice and strain into glasses.

Harry Lauder
½ Scotch Whisky
½ Sweet Vermouth
2 Dashes Sugar Syrup
Stir well with ice and strain into glass.

Highland Fling
1 Jigger Scotch Whisky
1 Teaspoon Sugar
2 Jiggers Milk
Shake very well with ice and strain into Delmonico glass. Sprinkle Nutmeg on top.

"Hoots Mon"
½ Scotch Whisky
¼ Lillet
¼ Sweet Vermouth
Stir well with ice and strain into glass.

Horse's Neck
1 Jigger American Whiskey
Rind of 1 Entire Lemon
Dash of Angostura (Optional)

Put into tall glass with ice. Fill with pale Ginger Ale. (Often made without Whiskey for a teetotaler's simulated highball.)

Hot Deck
¾ Rye Whiskey
¼ Sweet Vermouth
1 Dash Jamaica Ginger
Shake well with ice and strain into glass.

Hurricane
½ Jigger Rye or Bourbon Whiskey
½ Jigger White Crème de Menthe
½ Jigger Dry Gin
Juice of 1 Lemon
Shake well with ice and strain into glass.

Ink Street
½ Rye Whiskey
¼ Orange Juice
¼ Lemon Juice
Shake well with ice and strain into glass.

Irish
1 Jigger Irish Whiskey
2 Dashes Pernod
2 Dashes Curaçao
1 Dash Maraschino
1 Dash Angostura Bitters
Stir well with ice and strain. Squeeze Orange Peel on top.

John Wood (see Serpent's Tooth)

Kentucky Colonel
1 Jigger Bourbon
⅓ Jigger Benedictine
Stir with ice cubes.

King Cole
1 Jigger Bourbon Whiskey
1 Dash Fernet Branca
2 Dashes Sugar Syrup
1 Slice Orange
1 Slice Pineapple
1 Lump Ice
Muddle all ingredients well.

Kitchen Sink
¼ Rye Whiskey
¼ Gin
¼ Lemon Juice
¼ Orange Juice
1 Egg
1 Teaspoon Apricot Brandy
½ Teaspoon Powdered Sugar
Shake well with ice and strain
into glass.

Ladies'
1 Jigger Whiskey
2 Dashes Pernod
3 Dashes Anisette
1 Dash Angostura Bitters
Stir well with ice and strain into
glass. Serve with a piece of
Pineapple on top.

Lawhill
⅔ Rye Whiskey
⅓ Dry Vermouth
1 Dash Pernod
1 Dash Maraschino
1 Dash Angostura Bitters
Stir well with ice and strain
into glass.

Linstead (for 6)
6 Jiggers Whiskey
6 Jiggers Sweetened Pineapple
Juice
1 Dash Bitters
Shake well in ice and strain into
glasses. Squeeze Lemon Peel over
top.

Loch Lomond
1 Jigger Scotch Whisky
3 Dashes Angostura Bitters
1 Teaspoon Sugar
Shake well with ice and strain
into glass.

Los Angeles (for 4)
4 Large Jiggers Whiskey
Juice of 1 Lemon
4 Teaspoons Sugar
1 Egg
1 Dash Sweet Vermouth
Shake well with ice and strain
into glasses.

Mamie Taylor
1 Jigger Scotch
Juice of ½ Lime
Pour over ice in tall glass. Fill
with Ginger Ale or Ginger Beer.

Manhattan (Dry)
4 Parts Whiskey
1 Part Dry Vermouth
1 Dash Bitters
Stir very well with ice and strain
into glass. Add a twist of Lemon
Peel or a Cherry.

Manhattan (Perfect)
1 Jigger Bourbon
Dash Italian Vermouth
⅓ Jigger French Vermouth
Dash Angostura (optional)

Stir well with ice. For Perfect Rob Roy, substitute Scotch for Bourbon.

Manhattan (Sweet)
⅔ Whiskey
⅙ Sweet Vermouth
⅙ Dry Vermouth
1 Dash Bitters
Stir well with ice and strain into glass. Serve with a Cherry (optional).

Maple Leaf
1 Jigger Bourbon
1 Teaspoon Maple Syrup
Juice of ½ Lemon
Stir well over ice.

Master of the Hounds
1 Jigger Rye Whiskey
⅓ Jigger Cherry Brandy
2 Dashes Angostura Bitters
Stir well with ice and strain into glass.

Mickie Walker
3 Parts Scotch Whisky
1 Part Sweet Vermouth
1 Dash Lemon Juice
1 Dash Grenadine
Shake well with ice and strain into glass.

Millionaire No. 3
1 Jigger Bourbon
⅓ Jigger Curaçao
1 Egg White
1 Dash Grenadine
Shake well with shaved ice and strain into large cocktail glass.

Modern No. 2
2 Jiggers Scotch Whisky
1 Dash Lemon Juice
1 Dash Pernod
2 Dashes Jamaica Rum
1 Dash Orange Bitters
Stir well with ice, strain into glass and serve with a Cherry.

Monte Carlo
1 Jigger Rye Whiskey
⅓ Jigger Benedictine
2 Dashes Angostura Bitters
Shake well with ice and strain into glass.

Morning Glory
⅔ Jigger Whiskey
⅔ Jigger Brandy
1 Dash Pernod
2 Dashes Bitters
2 Dashes Curaçao
3 Dashes Sugar Syrup
1 Twist Lemon Peel
Place ingredients in large cocktail glass, with 1–2 pieces of ice. Stir and remove ice. Fill glass with Soda Water and stir with a teaspoon coated with Powdered Sugar.

Mountain
½ American Whiskey
⅙ Lemon Juice
⅙ Dry Vermouth
⅙ Sweet Vermouth
1 Egg White
Shake well with ice and strain into glass.

Mud Pie

In an Old-Fashioned glass muddle ½ cube Sugar with 2 dashes Peychaud's Bitters, 4 dashes Curaçao and 1 large cube ice. Decorate with fruit, if desired, and serve with 1 jigger Whiskey on the side.

New Orleans

1 Jigger Bourbon
1 Dash Orange Bitters
2 Dashes Angostura Bitters
1 Dash Anisette
2 Dashes Pernod
½ Lump Sugar
Stir well with ice and strain into glass. Serve with twist of Lemon Peel.

New York

1½ Jiggers American Whiskey
½ Teaspoon Powdered Sugar
1 Dash Grenadine
Juice of ½ Lime
1 Twist Orange Peel
Shake well with ice and strain into glass.

Oh, Henry!

⅓ Whiskey
⅓ Benedictine
⅓ Ginger Ale
Stir well with ice and strain into glass.

Old-Fashioned

Place in an Old-Fashioned glass 1 lump of Sugar. Sprinkle it with a light dash of Angostura Bitters.

Add ice cubes and twist of Lemon Peel (Maraschino Cherry and Orange Slice, if desired) and fill with Whiskey, any Whiskey.

Old Pal

⅓ Rye Whiskey
⅓ Dry Vermouth
⅓ Campari
Stir well with ice and strain into glass.

Old Pepper

1⅓ Jiggers Whiskey
Juice of ½ Lemon
1 Teaspoon Worcestershire Sauce
1 Teaspoon Chili Sauce
2 Dashes Angostura Bitters
1 Dash Tabasco Sauce
Shake well with ice and serve in Delmonico glass.

Old-Time Appetizer

½ Jigger Rye or Bourbon
½ Jigger Dubonnet
2 Dashes Curaçao
2 Dashes Pernod
1 Slice Orange
1 Slice Pineapple
1 Twist Lemon Peel
1 Dash Peychaud's Bitters
Place all together in Old-Fashioned glass with ice cubes, and serve with a muddler.

Opening

½ Rye Whiskey
¼ Sweet Vermouth
¼ Grenadine
Stir well with ice and strain into glass.

Oppenheim
½ Jigger Bourbon
¼ Jigger Grenadine
¼ Jigger Sweet Vermouth
Stir well with ice and strain into glass.

Oriental (see Derby)

Paddy
½ Irish Whiskey
½ Sweet Vermouth
1 Dash Angostura Bitters
Stir well with ice and strain into glass.

Palmer
1 Jigger American Whiskey
1 Dash Angostura Bitters
1 Dash Lemon Juice
Stir well with ice and strain into glass.

Pick-Up
⅔ American Whiskey
⅓ Fernet Branca
3 Dashes Pernod
1 Slice Lemon
Stir gently with a little ice and strain into glass.

Polly's Special
½ Scotch Whisky
¼ Unsweetened Grapefruit Juice
¼ Curaçao
Shake well with ice and strain into glass.

Quaker
½ American Whiskey
½ Brandy
1 Teaspoon Raspberry Syrup
Juice of ½ Lime

Shake well with ice and strain into glass.

Rah-Rah-Rut
1 Jigger Bourbon Whiskey
2 Dashes Pernod
2 Dashes Peychaud's Bitters
Stir well with ice and strain into glass.

Rattlesnake (for 6)
8 Jiggers American Whiskey
2 Egg Whites
2 Jiggers Sweetened Lemon Juice
3 Dashes Pernod
Shake well with ice and strain into glass.

Rob Roy
1 Jigger Scotch Whisky
⅔ Jigger Sweet Vermouth
2 Dashes Angostura Bitters
Stir well with ice and strain into glass. Serve with twist of Lemon Peel.

Rock and Rye
Dissolve 1 piece of Rock Candy in 2 jiggers of Rye Whiskey. Lemon Juice may be added if desired.

Russell House (Down the Hatch)
2 Jiggers American Whiskey
3 Dashes Blackberry Brandy
2 Dashes Sugar Syrup
2 Dashes Orange Bitters
Stir well with ice and strain into glass.

Rusty Nail
2 Parts Scotch
1 Part Drambuie or Lochan Ora
Serve chilled or not.

Rye Whiskey
2 Jiggers American Whiskey
4 Dashes Sugar Syrup
1 Dash Angostura Bitters
Stir well with ice and strain into
glass. Serve with a Cherry.

St. Nick's Coffee Cocktail
1 Jigger Scotch
2/3 Jigger Crème de Cacao
1 Teaspoon Sugar
1 Teaspoon Instant Coffee
2 Jiggers Cream
Stir well with ice.

Sazerac
1 Jigger American Whiskey
1 Dash Pernod
1 Dash Peychaud's Bitters
1 Lump Sugar, dissolved in 1
teaspoon Water
Stir well with ice and strain into
a chilled glass. Squeeze Lemon
Peel over top.

Scoff-Law
1/3 Rye Whiskey
1/3 Dry Vermouth
1/6 Lemon Juice
1/6 Grenadine
1 Dash Orange Bitters
Stir well with ice and strain into
glass.

Scotch Mist
Fill Old-Fashioned glass with
shaved ice. Pour in Scotch
Whisky as desired. Add twist of
Lemon Peel.
Note: Any Whiskey may be used.

Scotch-on-the-Rocks
Fill Old-Fashioned glass with ice
cubes. Pour in Whisky as
desired, with or without water,
and with or without twist of
Lemon Peel. Any Whiskey can be
served on-the-rocks.

Scotch Side Car
1 Jigger Scotch Whisky
1/2 Jigger Cointreau
1/2 Jigger Lemon Juice
Shake well with ice and strain
into large cocktail glass.
Note: Any Whiskey, Straight or
Blended, may be substituted.

Serpent's Tooth (John Wood)
2 Parts Irish Whiskey
4 Parts Sweet Vermouth
2 Parts Lemon Juice
1 Part Kümmel
1 Dash Angostura Bitters
Stir well with ice and strain into
glass.

"S.G."
1/3 Rye Whiskey
1/3 Lemon Juice
1/3 Orange Juice
1 Teaspoon Grenadine
Shake well with ice and strain
into glass.

Shamrock—Friendly Sons of St. Patrick
½ Irish Whiskey
½ Dry Vermouth
3 Dashes Green Chartreuse
3 Dashes Green Crème de Menthe
Stir well with ice and strain into glass. Serve with Green Olive.

Soul Kiss No. 2
⅓ Rye Whiskey
⅓ Dry Vermouth
⅙ Dubonnet
⅙ Orange Juice
1 Slice Orange
Stir well with ice and strain into glass.

Southside
Muddle in a mixing glass or shaker a few fresh Mint Leaves with 1 teaspoon Powdered Sugar. Add Juice of ½ Lemon and 1½ jiggers Bourbon. Shake thoroughly with ice and strain into glass.
Note: This may also be made with Gin.

S. S. Manhattan
½ Bourbon Whiskey
½ Orange Juice
1 Dash Benedictine
Shake well with ice and strain into glass.

Stone Fence No. 1 (see Long Drinks)

Temptation
1 Jigger Rye Whiskey
2 Dashes Curaçao
2 Dashes Pernod
2 Dashes Dubonnet
1 Twist each Orange and Lemon Peel
Stir well with ice and strain into glass.

Thistle
½ Scotch Whisky
½ Sweet Vermouth
2 Dashes Angostura Bitters
Stir well with ice and strain into glass.

Tipperary No. 2
⅓ Irish Whiskey
⅓ Chartreuse
⅓ Sweet Vermouth
Stir well with ice and strain into glass.

T.N.T.
½ American Whiskey
½ Pernod
Shake well with ice and strain into glass.

Tom Moore
⅔ Irish Whiskey
⅓ Sweet Vermouth
1 Dash Angostura Bitters
Stir well with ice and strain into glass.

Trilby No. 2
⅓ Scotch Whisky
⅓ Sweet Vermouth
⅓ Parfait Amour Liqueur
2 Dashes Orange Bitters
2 Dashes Pernod

Stir well with ice and strain into glass.

Up-to-Date
½ Rye Whiskey
½ Sherry
2 Dashes Angostura Bitters
2 Dashes Grand Marnier
Stir well with ice and strain into glass.

Waldorf No. 2
⅓ Bourbon Whiskey
⅓ Pernod
⅓ Sweet Vermouth
3 Dashes Angostura Bitters
Stir well with ice and strain into glass.

Ward Eight No. 2
1 Jigger Blended, Rye or Bourbon Whiskey
Juice ¼ Lemon or ½ Lime
2 or 4 Dashes Grenadine
Dash Orange Bitters (optional)
Shake well with ice and strain into goblet. Add extra ice and fruit garnish as desired. Serve with straws.

Wembley No. 2
⅓ Scotch Whisky
⅓ Dry Vermouth
⅓ Pineapple Juice
Shake well with ice and strain into glass.

Whiskey and Bitters
Same as WHISKEY, omitting Sugar Syrup. Generally served with ice in glass.

Whiskey and Honey
Place in Old-Fashioned glass 1 teaspoon Honey, 1 or 2 ice cubes, 1 twist Lemon Peel. Pour in 1 or 2 jiggers Whiskey. Serve with muddler and drink immediately.

Whiskey on Rocks
Place ice cubes in Old-Fashioned glass and pour in any Whiskey desired, with or without water.

Whiskey Sour
1 or 2 Jiggers any Whiskey
Juice of ½ Lemon
½ Teaspoon Sugar
Shake well with ice and serve in Delmonico glass, garnish with Cherry and Orange slice if desired. The proportion of Whiskey and Sugar may be altered to suit individual taste.

Whiskey Special (for 6)
6 Jiggers Whiskey
4 Jiggers Dry Vermouth
1 Jigger Orange Juice
1 Pinch Nutmeg
Shake well with ice and strain into glasses. Serve with a twist of Orange Peel.

Whisper
⅓ Whiskey
⅓ Dry Vermouth
⅓ Sweet Vermouth
Shake well with ice and strain into glass.

White Shadow
⅓ Rye Whiskey
⅓ Pernod
⅓ Cream

1 Pinch Nutmeg
Shake well with shaved ice and
strain into glass.

Whizz Bang
⅔ Scotch Whisky
⅓ Dry Vermouth
2 Dashes Orange Bitters
2 Dashes Grenadine
2 Dashes Pernod
Stir well with ice and strain into
glass.

Wild-Eyed Rose
2 Jiggers Irish Whiskey
½ Jigger Grenadine
Juice of ½ Lime
Place ingredients in large
cocktail glass with 1 ice cube and
fill with Soda Water.

Yashmak
⅓ Rye Whiskey
⅓ Pernod
⅓ Dry Vermouth
1 Dash Angostura Bitters
1 or 2 Pinches Sugar
Stir well with ice and strain into
glass.

Zazarac
⅓ Rye Whiskey
⅙ Sugar Syrup
⅙ Anisette
⅙ Light Rum
⅙ Pernod
1 Dash Orange Bitters
1 Dash Angostura Bitters
Shake well with ice and strain
into glass. Squeeze Lemon Peel
on top.

COLLINS

The Collins is generally made in
a highball glass. Its basic
proportions are 2 or 3 cubes of
ice, the juice of ½ or 1 Lemon,
1 or 1½ teaspoons Sugar and
1 or 2 jiggers of any of the
following liquors: Applejack,
Brandy, Gin, Rum, Whiskey or
Vodka.

The proportions are a matter of
personal taste, depending on the
strength and sweetness of drink
desired.

The TOM COLLINS is a GIN
COLLINS. The JOHN COLLINS
uses Holland Gin.

COOLERS

Applejack Cooler
1 Tablespoon Sugar
Juice of ½ Lemon
1 or 2 Jiggers Applejack
Shake well with cracked ice and strain into highball glass. Add ice cubes and fill with chilled Soda Water.

Apricot Cooler
1 Jigger Apricot Brandy
Juice of ½ each Lemon and Lime
2 Dashes Grenadine
Shake well with cracked ice and strain into highball glass and fill with Soda Water.

Bishop's Cooler
Place in large highball glass 2 jiggers Burgundy, ½ jigger Dark Rum, ⅓ jigger Orange Juice, ⅓ Lemon Juice, 1 teaspoon Sugar, 2 dashes Angostura Bitters. Fill with shaved ice, stir and serve.

Country Club Cooler
2 Jiggers Dry Vermouth
1 Teaspoon Grenadine
Place in tall glass with ice and fill with chilled Soda Water.

Cuban Cooler
Place ice cubes in a tall highball glass and add 1 or 2 jiggers Rum and fill with Ginger Ale. Garnish with twist of Lemon Peel.

Harvard Cooler
Place in a shaker with ice 1 tablespoon Sugar Syrup, juice of ½ Lemon and 1 or 2 jiggers Applejack. Shake well and strain into tall highball glass. Fill with chilled Soda Water.

Hawaiian Cooler
Place ice cubes in a large tumbler or highball glass and add a long twist of Orange Peel, 1 or 2 jiggers Rye Whiskey and fill with chilled Soda Water.

Highland Cooler
Place ice cubes in a tall glass and add 2 jiggers Scotch Whisky, 2 dashes Angostura Bitters, juice of ½ Lemon and 1 teaspoon Powdered Sugar. Stir and fill with chilled Ginger Ale.

Irish Cooler
Place ice cubes in a large tumbler or highball glass with a long twist of Lemon Peel. Add 1 or 2 jiggers Irish Whiskey and fill with Soda Water.

Lone Tree
The same as APRICOT COOLER, but with a little more Lemon Juice and a little less Grenadine.

Long Tom Cooler
The same as TOM COLLINS, but always with 1 slice of Orange.

Manhattan Cooler
Place in a tall glass 2 or 3 jiggers Claret, 3 dashes Rum, juice of ½ Lemon and 1 or 2 teaspoons Powdered Sugar. Add ice and decorate with fruit if desired.

Mint Cooler
Place ice in highball glass and add 2 jiggers Scotch Whisky, 3 dashes White Crème de Menthe and fill with Soda Water.

Moonlight
2 or 3 Jiggers Calvados or Applejack
Juice of 1 Lemon
1½ Teaspoons Sugar

Shake well with shaved ice and strain into tall glass. Fill with chilled Soda Water. Decorate with fruit if desired.

Orange Blossom Cooler
Shake well with shaved ice 1 or 2 jiggers Dry Gin, juice of ½ Orange, 1 teaspoon Sugar and strain into highball glass, filling with iced Soda Water. Garnish with fruit or Mint.

Red Wine Cooler
Dissolve 2 teaspoons Sugar in a very little water. Add 4 teaspoons Orange Juice and place in highball glass with ice cubes. Fill with any Red Wine and garnish with Lemon Slice.

Remsen Cooler
2 Jiggers Scotch Whisky or Dry Gin
1 Lemon
Soda Water
Peel off the rind of the Lemon in as long a twist as possible and place in highball glass with ice. Add liquor as desired and fill with Soda Water.

Scotch Cooler
Place in a highball glass 1 or 2 jiggers Scotch Whisky, 3 dashes Crème de Menthe and ice cubes. Fill with chilled Soda Water.

Scotch Stone Fence
Place 2 jiggers Scotch Whisky and 2 dashes Peychaud's Bitters in a highball glass with 1 small twist of Lemon Peel and ice cubes. Fill with Soda Water.

Sea Breeze
Place in a highball glass 1 jigger Dry Gin, 1 jigger Apricot Brandy, 1 dash Grenadine, juice of ½ Lemon and ice cubes. Fill with chilled Soda Water and decorate with sprigs of Mint.

Shady Grove
In a highball glass combine 2 jiggers Dry Gin, juice of ½ Lemon and 1½ teaspoons Sugar. Add ice cubes and fill with Ginger Beer.

Whiskey Cooler
Place in a highball glass 2 jiggers Rye or Bourbon, the juice of ½ Lemon, 1 teaspoon Sugar and ice cubes. Fill with chilled Ginger Ale.

White Wine Cooler
Place 1 tablespoon Sugar Syrup and 2 or 3 jiggers chilled Soda Water in a highball glass with ice cubes. Fill with chilled White Wine. Garnish with Mint and, if desired, an Orange slice.

Zenith
Place in a large tumbler several ice cubes with 1 tablespoon Pineapple Juice, 1 or 2 jiggers Dry Gin and fill with Soda Water. Serve with a Pineapple stick.

CRUSTAS

Basic
Crustas may be made of Applejack, Brandy, Gin, Rum or Whiskey. Rub the rim of a large Wineglass with Lemon, then dip glass in Powdered Sugar. Place in the glass a large twist of Lemon or Orange Peel and a Cherry. In a shaker with ice put 1 dash Angostura Bitters, 1 teaspoon each Lemon Juice and Maraschino and 1 or 2 jiggers of the desired liquor. Strain into prepared glass and serve.

CUPS

Burgundy Cup

2 Jiggers Whiskey
1 Jigger Curaçao
1 Jigger Benedictine
1½ Bottles Burgundy (Red)
1 Pint Soda Water
4 Tablespoons Sugar
Place in large pitcher with ice cubes and stir. Decorate with slices of Orange and Pineapple, Maraschino Cherries, Cucumber.

Chablis Cup

Place ice cubes in a large pitcher and add: 1 jigger Benedictine, 1 or 2 slices Lemon, 3 thin slices Pineapple, and 1 bottle Chablis (Pouilly or any White Burgundy may be used). Stir gently and serve. Peeled ripe Peaches may be used in place of Pineapple slices.

Cider Cup No. 1

1 Quart Cider
1 Jigger Maraschino
1 Jigger Curaçao
1 Jigger Brandy
Ice Cubes
Soda Water
Fill pitcher with ice cubes and decorate with Lemon or Orange Peel. Add other ingredients and Soda Water as desired.

Cider Cup No. 2 (for 4)

1 Quart Cider
1 Jigger Calvados or Apple

Brandy
1 Jigger Brandy
1 Jigger Curaçao
1 Pint Soda Water
Place all together in pitcher with ice cubes and 2 large sprigs Mint. Stir and serve.

Claret Cup (for 10)

1 Bottle Claret (Bordeaux)
½ Jigger Maraschino
½ Jigger Curaçao
1 Jigger Sugar Syrup
Decorate with Orange and Pineapple, and Mint if desired.

Claret Cup No. 2

Fill a large pitcher ½ full of cracked ice. Add 1 jigger Curaçao, 1 jigger Brandy, 1 jigger Sugar Syrup, 1 dash Maraschino, 1 Lemon, slicd thin, 1 Orange, sliced thin, 2 or 3 slices fresh Pineapple, ½ pint Soda Water, and 1 or 2 quarts Claret. Stir well. (It is advisable to add the Soda Water just before serving.) Makes 10 to 12 cups.

Empire Peach Cup

Carefully peel 1 or 2 ripe Peaches and slice into a large bowl or pitcher, losing as little juice as possible. Add 1 bottle Moselle and 2 or 3 tablespoons Sugar. Stir and set aside, covered, for ½ hour. Add 1 more bottle

Moselle and just before serving add ice and 1 bottle Sparkling Moselle. This Cup is perhaps better if no ice is added, but the pitcher or bowl should be set in a bed of crushed ice. Makes 15 to 20 cups.

Grapefruit Cup
Place a large piece of ice in a big pitcher or bowl and add 1 bottle Brandy, 2 jiggers Grenadine, meat of 3 seeded Grapefruits and 1 can of Grapefruit Juice. Stir and decorate with Mint Leaves. Just before serving, add 1 small bottle Soda Water. 10 to 12 cups.

Kalte Ente
Place in a larg pitcher the whole curled rind of 1 Lemon, 2 jiggers Curaçao, 1 bottle Moselle, chilled, and 1 bottle Sparkling Moselle. 10 to 12 cups.

May Wine
In a large pitcher soak a bunch of Woodruff in 3 bottles Moselle for 1 hour, with a piece of ice. Add 6 lumps Sugar, 2 jiggers Curaçao, 2 jiggers Brandy and 1 bottle Sparkling Moselle before serving. 25 to 30 cups.

Moselle Cup
Place in a large pitcher a good piece of ice, 3 peeled ripe Peaches, quartered, 12 Maraschino Cherries, 1 jigger Benedictine, 1 bottle Moselle

and, just before serving, 1 ice-cold bottle Sparkling Moselle. 10 to 12 cups.

Pfirsich Bowle
Place a large chunk of ice in a big pitcher, with 2 whole ripe Peaches which have been pierced with a fork. Add 1 or 2 bottles light Rhine Wine and Powdered Sugar, if desired. Mint may also be added. 10 to 12 cups.

Rhine Wine Cup
Place a large piece of ice in a big pitcher or punch bowl with slices of Orange, Pineapple, Cucumber Peel and a few Maraschino Cherries. Add 1 jigger Maraschino, 1 jigger Curaçao, 2 bottles Rhine Wine. 10 to 12 cups.

Sauterne Cup
Place a large pitcher or punch bowl in a bed of crushed ice. Combine the ingredients in the order listed:
1 Jigger Brandy
1 Jigger Curaçao
1 Jigger Maraschino
2 Bottles Sauterne, chilled
½ Pint chilled Soda Water
Garnish with Lemon and Orange slices. Serves 10 to 12.

Velvet Cup
Prepare same as CHAMPAGNE VELVET, but in a pitcher with ice, pouring in Stout and Champagne carefully so as not to overflow.

DAISIES

Note: Daisies are overgrown Cocktails. They should be served in very large cocktail glasses or goblets. Place the juice of ½ Lemon, 1 teaspoon Grenadine and 1 or 2 jiggers of Applejack, Brandy, Gin, Rum or Whiskey in a shaker with shaved ice. Shake well and strain into glass. Fill with chilled Soda Water. Sometimes the White of 1 Egg and a dash of Pernod are added.

Santa Cruz Rum Daisy
Fill a goblet ⅓ full of shaved ice and add 3 dashes Sugar Syrup, 3 dashes Maraschino or Curaçao, juice of ½ Lemon and fill with Rum.

FIXES

All Fixes should be served in small tumblers with shaved ice.

Brandy Fix
1 Jigger Brandy
1 Jigger Cherry Brandy
1 Teaspoon Sugar
1 Teaspoon Water
Juice of ½ Lemon
Moisten the Sugar with the Water and add the other ingredients. Fill with ice and stir gently. Add a slice of Lemon or twist of Peel. Serve with a straw.

Gin Fix
2 Jiggers Dry Gin
1 Teaspoon Sugar
1 Teaspoon Water
Juice of ½ Lemon
Moisten the Sugar with the Water and add other ingredients. Fill with ice and stir gently. Add a slice of Lemon or twist of Peel. Serve with a straw.
Note: The RUM FIX and the WHISKEY FIX are made as above, substituting the desired liquor.

Santa Cruz Fix
The SANTA CRUZ FIX is made the same as the BRANDY FIX, substituting Rum for the Brandy.

FIZZES

Most Fizzes are served in a 7-ounce highball glass.

Alabama Fizz
Prepare the same as GIN FIZZ, adding a sprig of Mint.

Albemarle
2 Jiggers Dry Gin
½ Tablespoon Powdered Sugar
1 Dash Raspberry Syrup
Juice of ½ Lemon
Shake well with ice and strain into glass. Fill with Soda Water.

American Fizz
1 Jigger Gin
1 Jigger Brandy
Juice of ½ Lemon
1 Teaspoon Grenadine
Shake well with ice and strain into glass.

Apple Blow
2 Jiggers Applejack
4 Dashes Lemon Juice
1 Teaspoon Sugar
1 Egg White
Shake well with ice and strain into glass. Fill with Soda Water.

Bacardi Fizz
2 Jiggers Bacardi Rum
1 Teaspoon Sugar
Juice of ½ Lemon
Shake well with ice and strain into glass. Fill with Soda Water.

Bismarck Fizz (Sloe Gin Fizz)
2 Jiggers Sloe Gin
Juice of ½ Lemon
Shake well with ice and strain into glass. Fill with Soda Water.

Boot Leg
Make same as GIN FIZZ, adding white of 1 Egg and sprigs of Mint.

Brandy Fizz
Make same as GIN FIZZ, using Brandy.

Broadmoor Cooler
1 Jigger Gin
1 Jigger Green Crème de Menthe
Pour into highball glass with cracked ice; fill with Fresca.

Bucks Fizz
1 Jigger Gin
½ Teaspoon Sugar
Juice of ½ Orange
Shake well with ice and strain into glass. Fill with chilled Champagne.

Cider Fizz (for 2)
2 Jiggers Gold Label Rum
¼ Cup Apple Cider
1 Tablespoon Lemon Juice
1 Teaspoon Sugar
½ Cup Shaved Ice
Pre-chill the ingredients and place them in the glass container

of an electric blender. Cover and turn on for 20 seconds. Place two ice cubes in large highball glasses. Pour in blended mixture and fill with Soda Water or Ginger Ale.

Cream Fizz
Make same as GIN FIZZ with 1 or 2 teaspoons Cream added.

Derby Fizz
1 Jigger Whiskey
5 Dashes Lemon Juice
1 Teaspoon Sugar
1 Egg
3 Dashes Curaçao
Shake well with ice and strain into glass. Fill up with Soda Water.

Diamond Fizz
1 Jigger Gin
½ Teaspoon Sugar
Juice of ½ Lemon
Shake well with ice and strain into glass. Fill up with Soda Water.

Dubonnet Fizz
2 Jiggers Dubonnet
1 Teaspoon Cherry Brandy
Juice of ½ Orange
Juice of ¼ Lemon
Shake well with ice and strain into glass. Fill up with Soda Water.

Frank's Special Fizz
2 Jiggers Gin
¼ Crushed Peach
½ Teaspoon Sugar
Juice of ½ Lemon

Shake well with ice and strain into glass. Fill with Soda Water or chilled Champagne.

Gin Fizz
2 Jiggers Dry Gin
1 Tablespoon Powdered Sugar
Juice of ½ Lemon
Juice of ½ Lime
Shake well with ice and strain into glass. Fill up with Soda Water.

Gin and Tonic
2 Jiggers Gin
Lemon Juice
Pour over ice in a tall glass; fill up with Tonic (Quinine Water).

Golden Fizz
Make same as GIN FIZZ, adding Yolk of 1 Egg.

Grand Royal Fizz
Make same as GIN FIZZ, adding 1 dash Maraschino, 3 dashes Orange Juice and ½ jigger Cream.

Grenadine Fizz
2 Jiggers Gin
2 Teaspoons Grenadine
Juice of ½ Lemon
Shake well with ice and strain into glass. Fill up with Soda Water.

Hoffman House Fizz
2 Jiggers Dry Gin
Juice of ½ Lemon
1 Teaspoon Sugar
1 Teaspoon Cream
2 Dashes Maraschino

Shake well with ice and strain
into glass. Fill up with Soda
Water.

Holland Gin Fizz
Make same as GIN FIZZ, using
Holland Gin.

Imperial Fizz
1 Jigger Rye or Bourbon Whiskey
Juice of ½ Lemon
½ Teaspoon Sugar
Shake well with ice and strain
into glass. Fill with chilled
Champagne.

Imperial Hotel Fizz
⅔ Whiskey
⅓ Light Rum
4 Dashes Lemon Juice
Juice of ½ Lime
Shake well with ice and strain
into glass. Fill with Soda Water.

Irish Fizz
2 Jiggers Irish Whiskey
1 Teaspoon Curaçao
½ Teaspoon Sugar
Juice of ½ Lemon
Shake well with ice and strain
into glass. Fill up with Soda
Water.

Jubilee Fizz
½ Dry Gin
½ Unsweetened Pineapple
Juice
Shake well with ice and strain
into glass. Fill with chilled
Champagne.

May Blossom Fizz
1 Jigger Swedish Punch
1 Teaspoon Grenadine
Juice of ½ Lemon
Shake well with ice and strain
into glass. Fill up with Soda
Water.

Morning Glory Fizz
2 Jiggers Scotch Whisky
2 Dashes Pernod
1 Egg White
1 Teaspoon Powdered Sugar
Juice of ½ Lemon
Juice of ½ Lime
Shake well with ice and strain
into glass. Fill up with Soda
Water.

New Orleans Fizz
2 Jiggers Dry Gin
1 Egg White
Juice of ½ Lemon
1 Teaspoon Sugar
1 Teaspoon Cream
1 Dash Orange Flower Water
Shake well with ice and strain
into glass. Fill with Soda Water.

Nicky's Fizz
2 Jiggers Dry Gin
1 Jigger Sweetened Grapefruit
Juice
Shake well with ice and strain
into glass. Fill up with Soda
Water.

Orange Fizz No. 1
2 Jiggers Dry Gin
Juice of ½ Orange
1 Dash Grenadine

Shake well with ice and strain into glass. Fill up with Soda Water.

Orange Fizz No. 2

2 Jiggers Dry Gin
Juice of ½ Orange
Juice of ½ Lime
Juice of ¼ Lemon
Shake well with ice and strain into glass. Fill up with Soda Water.

Ostend Fizz

1 Jigger Crème de Cassis
1 Jigger Kirsch
Shake well with ice and strain into glass. Fill up with Soda Water.

Peach Blow Fizz

2 Jiggers Dry Gin
⅔ Jigger Cream
1 Teaspoon Powdered Sugar
4 Mashed Strawberries
Juice of ½ Lemon
Juice of ½ Lime
Shake well with ice and strain into glass. Fill up with Soda Water.

Pineapple Fizz

2 Jiggers Light Rum
½ Tablespoon Powdered Sugar
2 Tablespoons Pineapple Juice
1 Dash Lime Juice
Shake well with ice and strain into glass. Fill up with Soda Water.
Note: Gin may be used instead of Rum if desired.

Ramoz (Ramos) Fizz

1½ Jiggers Dry Gin
1 Egg White
⅔ Jigger Cream
3 Dashes Orange Flower Water
Juice of ½ Lime
Juice of ½ Lemon
Shake well with ice and pour into 10-ounce glass with the edge frosted with Lemon and Sugar. Add Soda Water if desired.

Rose in June Fizz

1 Jigger Gin
1 Jigger Framboise
Juice of 1 Orange
Juice of 2 Limes
Shake well with ice and strain into glass. Add several dashes of Soda Water.

Royal Fizz

1 Jigger Gin
1 Egg
1 Teaspoon Sugar
Juice of ½ Lemon
Shake well with ice and strain into glass. Fill up with Soda Water.

Ruby Fizz

2 Jiggers Sloe Gin
1 Egg White
1 Teaspoon Raspberry Syrup
Juice of ½ Lemon
Shake well with ice and strain into glass. Fill up with Soda Water.

Rum Fizz

1 Jigger Rum
½ Jigger Cherry Brandy
½ Teaspoon Sugar
Juice of ½ Lemon

Shake well with ice and strain into glass. Fill up with Soda Water.

Safari Cooler
(An African drink originally made with Waragi, an African-made Gin)
1 Jigger Gin
Lemon Slice
Dash Angostura
Pour into large glass with cracked ice; fill with Ginger Beer.

Saratoga Fizz
1 Jigger Rye or Bourbon Whiskey
1/3 Jigger Lemon Juice
1 Teaspoon Lime Juice
1 Teaspoon Sugar
1 Egg White
Shake well with ice and pour into glass. Garnish with a Cherry.

Scotch Fizz
Make same as GIN FIZZ, using Scotch Whisky in place of Gin.

Seapea Fizz
2 Jiggers Pernod
Juice of 1/2 Lemon
Shake well with ice and strain into glass. Fill up with Soda Water.

Silver Ball Fizz
2 Jiggers Rhine Wine
2 Dashes Orange Flower Water
1 Teaspoon Powdered Sugar
1 Egg White
1 Jigger Grapefruit Juice

Shake well with ice and strain into glass. Fill up with Soda Water.

Silver Fizz
Make same as GIN FIZZ, adding White of 1 Egg.

Sloe Gin Fizz (see Bismarck Fizz)

Southside Fizz
Make same as GIN FIZZ, with Mint Leaves added.

Strawberry Fizz
1 Jigger Gin
4 Crushed Strawberries
1/2 Teaspoon Sugar
Juice of 1/2 Lemon
Shake well with ice and strain into glass. Fill up with Soda Water.

Texas Fizz
1 Jigger Gin
1 Dash Grenadine
Juice of 1/4 Orange
Juice of 1/4 Lemon
Shake well with ice and strain into glass. Fill up with chilled Champagne.

Violet Fizz
1 Jigger Dry Gin
1 Teaspoon Raspberry Syrup
1 Teaspoon Cream
Juice of 1/2 Lemon
Shake well with ice and strain into glass. Fill up with Soda Water.

FLIPS

Applejack Flip (for 2)
2⅔ Jiggers Applejack
1 Egg
2 Teaspoons Sugar
½ Cup Shaved Ice
Chill all ingredients and place in
chilled container of electric
blender. Cover and blend for 20
seconds. Pour into 6-ounce
glasses and sprinkle with Nutmeg.

Blackberry Flip
2 Jiggers Blackberry Brandy
1 Egg
1 Teaspoon Powdered Sugar
Shake well with cracked ice and
strain into glass. Sprinkle
Nutmeg on top.

Boston Flip
Place in a shaker 1 Egg, 1
teaspoon Sugar, 1 jigger
Madeira, and 1 jigger Rye
Whiskey. Shake well with ice
and strain into large cocktail
glass. Sprinkle with Nutmeg.

Brandy Flip
Prepare same as BLACKBERRY
FLIP.

Cherry Brandy Flip
Prepare same as BLACKBERRY
FLIP.

Claret Flip (for 2)
⅓ Cup Claret
1 Egg
1 Teaspoon Sugar
1 Dash Angostura Bitters
½ Cup Shaved Ice
Follow directions for preparation
of APPLEJACK FLIP.

Muscatel Flip (for 2)
1⅓ Jiggers Brandy
¼ Cup Muscatel Wine
1 Egg
1 Teaspoon Sugar
1 Tablespoon Cream
½ Cup Shaved Ice
Follow directions for preparation
of APPLEJACK FLIP.

Port Flip
Prepare as same as BLACKBERRY
FLIP, adding 1 or 2 dashes
Benedictine.

Rum Flip
Prepare same as BLACKBERRY
FLIP.

Sherry Flip
Prepare same as BLACKBERRY
FLIP.

Whiskey Flip
Prepare same as BLACKBERRY
FLIP, adding 2 or 3 dashes Rum.

Whiskey Peppermint Flip
Make same as BLACKBERRY FLIP,
adding ⅓ jigger Peppermint.

FLOATS

Brandy Float
Place 1 or 2 cubes of Ice in an Old-Fashioned glass and fill it nearly full of chilled Soda Water. Lay the bowl of a teaspoon just at the top and pour in Brandy carefully so that it flows out over the surface but does not mix. The amount of Brandy is optional. Rum or any Whiskey may be substituted for the Brandy.

Liqueur Float
Fill a Liqueur glass almost full of any Liqueur you desire. Pour in Cream carefully so that it floats on top.

FRAPPÉS

Frappés may be made in three ways and of any Liquor or Liqueur—or Combination—you desire.
1. Fill a cocktail glass with shaved Ice and pour in the Liquor. Serve with a straw.
2. Fill a shaker about half full of shaved Ice, add the Liquor, shake thoroughly and strain into glass.
3. Blend shaved Ice and Liquor or Liqueur together in an electric blender and pour unstrained into glass.

HOT DRINKS

Ale Flip (for 4)

Place 1 quart of Ale in a saucepan on the fire and let it come to a boil. Have ready the Whites of 2 Eggs and the Yolks of 4, well beaten separately. Add them bit by bit to 4 tablespoons Sugar which has been moistened with a little Water and sprinkled with ½ teaspoon Nutmeg. When all are mixed, pour in the hot Ale, beating as you do so; and then pour from the original bowl into another one and backwards and forwards several times till the Flip is smooth and frothy.

Apple Toddy

Place ¼ Baked Apple in a glass with 1 teaspoon Powdered Sugar and 2 jiggers Calvados or Applejack. Fill glass with Boiling Water and serve with grating of Nutmeg.

Black Stripe

Place 1 teaspoon Molasses in a heated tumbler with 2 jiggers Dark Rum and a twist of Lemon Peel. Add Boiling Water. Stir and serve.

Blue Blazer

This drink requires 2 good-sized mugs with handles. Put 2 jiggers Scotch Whisky in 1 mug and 2 jiggers Boiling Water in the other. Blaze the Scotch and while it is blazing, pour the ingredients back and forth from 1 mug to the other. If you do this properly it will look like a stream of fire. Add 1 teaspoon fine grain Sugar and serve in a heated tumbler with a twist of Lemon Peel.

Brandy Blazer

Combine in a small thick glass
2 jiggers Brandy, 1 lump Sugar
and 1 twist of Orange Peel.
Blaze the Brandy and stir with a
long spoon. Strain into cocktail
glass and serve.

Brandy Toddy

Dissolve 1 lump of Sugar in a
tumbler with a little Water and
add 2 jiggers Brandy, a twist of
Lemon Peel and fill with Boiling
Water. Stir and serve.

Café Brûlot

8 Lumps Sugar
6 Jiggers Cognac
2 Sticks Cinnamon, broken
1 Twist Lmon Peel
12 Whole Cloves
2 Large Twists Orange Peel
5 Demi-tasse Cups of Strong
Black Coffee
Place all ingredients, except
Coffee, in a Chafing-Dish. Heat
gently, stirring constantly with
a metal ladle, until well warmed.
Blaze and let burn about 1
minute. Slowly pour in the black
Coffee. Ladle into Demi-tasse
cups and serve.

Café Brûlot Cocktail

Moisten the edge of a heavy
glass with a piece of Lemon. Dip
in Powdered Sugar and add
about 3 jiggers hot Coffee. Float
⅔ jigger Brandy on top. Blaze
and serve.

Café Diable

This is essentially the same as
CAFÉ BRÛLOT but requires a
longer blazing period.

Café Royale

Place a lump of Sugar in a spoon
and balance over a Demi-tasse
cup of hot black Coffee. Fill the
spoon with Brandy and when
warm, blaze. As the flame begins
to fade pour the contents into
the Coffee.

Christmas Punch No. 1

Combine in a large saucepan or
heatproof dish 2 bottles of
Brandy, 2 bottles Champagne,
1 pound of Sugar and 1 pound
of cubed fresh Pineapple. Heat
to a foam but do not boil. Pour
Brandy on top and blaze. Let
burn for 1 minute and ladle into
heated Wineglasses.

Columbia Skin

Heat in a small saucepan 1
tablespoon Water, 2 lumps of
Sugar, the Juice of ½ Lemon,
1 teaspoon Curaçao and 2 jiggers
Rum. Let foam but do not boil.
Serve in heated Wineglass.
Note: Brandy, Gin or Whiskey
may be prepared as above.

English Bishop (for about 6)

Stick an Orange generously with
Cloves and sprinkle it with
Brown Sugar. Place it in a
medium hot oven until
moderately browned. Quarter it
and place it in a heavy saucepan
with 1 quart of hot Port.

Simmer about 20 minutes and ladle into heated Punch glasses. Add ½ jigger Brandy to each glass before serving.

Farmer's Bishop (for 15–20)
1 Fifth Apple Brandy
2 Quarts Cider
5 Oranges Stuck with Cloves
Sticks of Cinnamon, One for Each Mug or Cup
Warm the Brandy and the Cider by immersing the bottles in hot water. Do not boil. Roast the Oranges at 300° for 25 minutes. In a *metal* punch bowl or pot put the Oranges and pour the hot Brandy over. Ignite. Let burn just a few minutes (with dimmed lights to enjoy the spectacle). Then douse blue flame with hot Cider. Pour into mugs or cups with Cinnamon Stick stirrer.

Festival Punch (for about 10)
1 Quart Jamaica Rum
1 Quart Sweet Apple Cider
2 or 3 Sticks Cinnamon, broken
2 Teaspoons Ground Allspice
1 or 2 Tablespoons Butter
Heat ingredients in a heavy saucepan until almost boiling. Serve hot in mugs.

Glögg (for 12)
¾ Cup Granulated Sugar
⅔ Jigger Angostura Bitters
6 Jiggers Claret
6 Jiggers Sherry
3 Jiggers Brandy
Heat all ingredients in a heavy saucepan. Place spoons in heated Old-Fashioned glasses and pour ¾ full with the hot mixture.

Hot Benefactor
Place in a heated tumbler 2 lumps Sugar, dissolved with a little Boiling Water. Add 2 jiggers each Jamaica Rum and Burgundy. Fill with Boiling Water and serve with a slice of Lemon and a grating of Nutmeg.

Hot Buttered Rum
2 Jiggers Jamaica Rum
1 Twist Lemon Peel
1 Stick Cinnamon
1 or 2 Cloves
Boiling Cider
Butter
Place Rum, Lemon Peel, Clove and Cinnamon in a Pewter Tankard or heavy mug. Fill with Boiling Cider. Float a pat of Butter on top and stir well.

Hot Gin
2 Jiggers Gin
1 or 2 lumps Sugar
Juice of ½ Lemon
Place in small tumbler and fill with Hot Water. Serve with a spoon.

Hot Lemonade
This is made the same as LEMONADE (Plain)—see Index —using Hot Water instead of the chilled Soda. Frequently a jigger of Whiskey, Brandy or Rum is added.

Hot Locomotive
1 Egg Yolk
1½ Teaspoons Sugar
⅔ Jigger Honey
4 Jiggers Burgundy or Claret
⅓ Jigger Curaçao

Blend Egg Yolk, Sugar and
Honey in a small saucepan. Add
Wine and Curaçao and heat to
the simmering point. Pour back
and forth several times into a
heated mug. Serve with a thin
Lemon slice and pinch of
Cinnamon.

Hot Milk Punch
1 Jigger Light Rum
1 Jigger Brandy
1 Teaspoon Sugar
Hot Milk
Combine the Sugar, Rum and
Brandy in a tall glass. Fill with
Hot Milk. Stir and top with
Nutmeg.

Hot Rum Bowl
(for approximately 16)
1 Quart Jamaica Rum
3 Quarts Sweet Apple Cider
1 Cup Brown Sugar
1 Cup Boiling Water
Butter
Nutmeg
In a saucepan dissolve Sugar in
Boiling Water. Add Cider and
heat. Add Rum and 1 or 2
generous teaspoons Butter. Place
in a heated bowl and sprinkle
with Nutmeg. Serve in mugs.

Hot Rum Lemonade
Combine 1 teaspoon Sugar, the
Juice of ½ Lemon and 1 jigger
Rum in a heated tumbler or mug.
Add freshly Boiling Water and a
slice of Lemon.

Hot Rye
In a small tumbler dissolve 1
lump Sugar in a very little Hot
Water. Add 1 small piece
Cinnamon, 1 twist Lemon Peel
and 2 jiggers Rye Whiskey. Serve
Hot Water in a pitcher on the
side, to be added as desired.

Hot Scotch
Prepare same as HOT RYE.

Hot Toddies
⅔ Jigger Applejack, Brandy,
Rum or any Whiskey
1 Teaspoon Sugar
2 Cloves
1 Slice Lemon
Place ingredients in Old-
Fashioned glass with a silver
spoon and fill with Boiling
Water. A small piece of
Cinnamon may be added if
desired.

Hot Toddy Bowl (for about 16)
1 Quart Applejack, Brandy,
Rum or any Whiskey
2 Quarts Boiling Water
1 Whole Lemon
Whole Cloves
Sugar Syrup to taste
Stud the Lemon with whole
Cloves and slice it as thin as
possible. Combine the Liquor,
Sugar Syrup to taste and Lemon
Slices in a heated bowl. Add the
Boiling Water and serve in hot
mugs with a Lemon slice in each
serving. Cinnamon may be added
if desired.

Hot Wine Lemonade

1 Jigger Red Wine
Juice of ½ or 1 Lemon
1½ Teaspoons Sugar
Twist of Lemon Peel
Combine Sugar, Juice and Wine in a hot tumbler or mug. Add Boiling Water and twist of Lemon Peel.

Jersey Flamer (for 8)

1 Quart Applejack
⅔ Jigger Angostura Bitters
1 Cup Sugar
2 Large Twists Lemon Peel
1 Quart Boiling Water
Combine in saucepan the Applejack, Bitters, Sugar and Lemon Peel. Heat slightly and stir to dissolve the Sugar. Turn into a heated heatproof bowl. Blaze and while blazing, pour on Boiling Water. Serve in heated mugs.

Jersey Mug

Place in a heated mug 2 jiggers Applejack, 1 good dash Angostura Bitters, several whole Cloves and a large twist of Lemon Peel. Fill with Boiling Water and float Applejack on top. Blaze and serve.

Mariner's Grog

1 Jigger Jamaica Rum
1 Lump Sugar
Several Cloves
1 Small Stick Cinnamon
Juice of ½ Lemon
1 Slice Lemon

Place all ingredients in a heavy mug. Fill with Boiling Water and stir and serve.

Mulled Wine

2½ Jiggers Claret or any other Red Wine
5 Jiggers Water
1 Dash Angostura Bitters
1 Teaspoon Sugar
1 Large Twist Lemon Peel
1 Pinch Allspice
1 Small Piece Cinnamon
Several Cloves
Heat all together in a saucepan but do not boil. Place a silver spoon in a large tumbler and strain in the mixture.
Note: MULLED CIDER may be prepared the same way, using 7 jiggers Cider instead of Wine and Water. A dash of Rum may be added.

Negus

Heat 1 bottle of Sherry or Port and place in a pitcher. Rub a little Lemon Rind on 6 cubes of Sugar and add to the mixture. Also add 2–3 large twists of Rind and the Juice of 1 Lemon. Add 10 drops of Vanilla and 2 cups of Boiling Water. Sweeten to taste if necessary and strain into glasses. Add a grating of Nutmeg and serve. Makes 8 cups.

Tom and Jerry

12 Eggs
6 Tablespoons Granulated Sugar
1 Teaspoon Grated Nutmeg
Rum
Bourbon or Rye
Hot Milk or Boiling Water

Beat the Eggs until thick and light in color. Gradually add the Sugar and Nutmeg and continue beating until the batter is very thick. Chill for several hours. To serve, put 1 heaping tablespoon of the batter into a warm mug. Add ½ jigger Rum and 1 jigger Bourbon or Rye. Fill the mug with hot milk or boiling water as desired. Stir and serve with a light grating of Nutmeg on top. More Liquor may be used if desired but in the same proportion as above.

Wassail
12 Eggs
4 Bottles Sherry or Madeira
2 Pounds Sugar
1 Teaspoon Powdered Nutmeg
2 Teaspoons Ginger
6 Whole Cloves
½ Teaspoon Mace
6 Whole Allspice
1 Teaspoon Cinnamon
Mix the dry ingredients in ½ pint of Water. Add the Wine and let the mixture simmer over a very slow fire. Beat the Egg Yolks and Whites separately and add these to the hot brew. Before serving, add several Baked Apples and lace the mixture well with Brandy. Makes 25 to 30 cups.

Whiskey Lemonade
Prepare same as HOT RUM LEMONADE, substituting Whiskey for Rum.

JULEPS

You will rarely find two people in any gathering who will agree as to what is or what is not a proper MINT JULEP. The recipe given is certainly an easy one to follow and is as good as they come.

Mint Julep
2 Jiggers Bourbon
1 Teaspoon Powdered Sugar
Mint
Soda Water
Fill a Collins glass with crushed ice and set it aside. Strip the leaves from 2 sprigs of Mint and muddle them in a small glass with the Sugar. Add a small splash of Soda Water, muddle again and add the Bourbon. Stir and strain into the prepared glass over the ice. Work a long-handled spoon up and down in the mixture until the outside of the glass begins to frost. Decorate with sprigs of Mint. Add more Whiskey if desired. Sometimes the Julep is topped with a splash of Rum.

Note: This same Julep may be made with Applejack, Brandy, Gin, Rum or Rye Whiskey. A CHAMPAGNE JULEP is also delicious but when making one, more Champagne will be needed and perhaps a dash of Brandy added. The GIN MINT JULEP is frequently called a MAJOR BAILEY and may be served as a cocktail.

LONG DRINKS

Americano
Place in a tumbler 2 jiggers Sweet Vermouth and 1 jigger Campari. Add 2 ice cubes and a twist of Lemon Peel. Fill with Soda Water.

American Punch
2/3 Jigger Brandy
2/3 Jigger Dry Vermouth
1 Teaspoon Crème de Menthe
Juice of 1/2 Orange
1/2 Teaspoon Sugar
Shake Juice, Sugar, Brandy and Vermouth with cracked ice. Strain into 10-ounce glass or large goblet filled with shaved ice and the Crème de Menthe.

American Rose
1 Jigger Brandy
1 Dash Pernod
1 Teaspoon Grenadine
2 Slices of Ripe Peach, crushed with a fork
Shake in a shaker with crushed ice and strain into 10-ounce glass. Fill with chilled Champagne.

Angostura Highball
Place in a tumbler 2 cubes of ice, 1 teaspoon Angostura Bitters and fill up with Ginger Ale.

Bermuda Highball
3/4 Jigger Dry Gin
3/4 Jigger Brandy
1/2 Jigger Dry Vermouth
Combine ingredients in highball glass, with ice cubes, and fill with Ginger Ale or Soda Water. Garnish with Lemon Peel and serve.

Bishop
Fill a tumbler 1/2 full with cracked ice. Add 1 teaspoon Sugar, Juice of 1/2 Lemon, Juice of 1/2 Orange and fill with Burgundy or Claret. Stir and add 1 slice of Orange and several dashes of Rum.

Black Rose

In a tumbler or highball glass, with 2 cubes of ice, place 1 teaspoon Sugar, 1 jigger St. James Rum and fill with cold black coffee. Stir and serve.

Byrrh Cassis

Combine in a tumbler or highball glass, with 2 cubes of ice, 1 teaspoon Crème de Cassis and 2 jiggers Byrrh. Fill with Soda Water, stir and serve.

California Lemonade

1 Jigger Rye Whiskey
1 Dash Grenadine
Juice of 1 Lemon
Juice of 1 Lime
1 Tablespoon Powdered Sugar
Shake well with ice and strain into glass. Fill with chilled Soda Water.

Cassisco

Place 2 cubes of ice in a tumbler or large goblet. Add 1 tablespoon Crème de Cassis and 1 jigger Brandy. Fill with Soda Water and serve.

Cincinnati

Fill a highball glass 1/2 full of Beer. Fill up with chilled Soda Water and serve.

Cloak and Dagger

Fill a highball glass with ice cubes. Add 1 1/2 jiggers Jamaica Rum and fill with Cola. Add a generous twist of Orange Peel and a dash of Orange Bitters.

Cocoa Rickey

Place a scoop of Vanilla Ice Cream in a large highball glass. Add 1 jigger Crème de Cacao, 1 tablespoon Milk and fill with Soda Water. Stir and add Sugar if necessary.

Corpse Reviver No. 3

Place 1 or 2 ice cubes in a highball glass and add the Juice of 1/4 Lemon, 1 jigger Pernod and fill with chilled Champagne. Stir and serve.

Cuba Libre

Place 2 or 3 ice cubes in a large highball glass. Add 2 jiggers Rum, the Juice of 1/2 Lime and fill with Cola.

Doctor Funk

1 2/3 Jiggers Martinique Rum
1/8 Jigger Pernod
1/3 Jigger Lemon Juice
1/8 Jigger Grenadine
1/4 Teaspoon Sugar
1 Lime
Cut Lime in half and squeeze into shaker, dropping in the Rinds also. Add all other ingredients and shake with crushed ice. Pour into 12-ounce glass and if necessary fill with Soda Water. Decorate with fruit if desired.

Dog's Nose

Place 1 or 2 jiggers Gin in a tall highball glass. Fill up with cold Beer or Stout.

El Diabolo
1 Jigger Tequila
1/3 Jigger Crème de Cassis
1/2 Lime
Ginger Ale
Squeeze and drop the Lime into highball glass. Add ice and other ingredients and fill with Ginger Ale.

Florida Special No. 2
2 Jiggers Gin
Juice of 1/2 Orange
Rind of Whole Orange, cut in spiral form
Place Orange Rind in tall glass and add ice and other ingredients. Fill with Ginger Ale.

Fog Cutter
1 1/3 Jiggers Puerto Rican Rum
2/3 Jigger Brandy
1/3 Jigger Gin
2/3 Jigger Orange Juice
1 Jigger Lemon Juice
1/3 Jigger Orgeat Syrup
Sherry
Shake all the ingredients, except the Sherry, with cracked ice and pour into a 14-ounce glass with the ice. Float the Sherry on top and serve with straws.

Fog Horn
Place 2 cubes of ice in a highball glass. Add 2 jiggers Dry Gin and 1 slice of Lemon. Fill with Ginger Beer and serve.

Frank's Refresher
Combine in a tumbler or highball glass, with 2 cubes of ice, the Juice of 1/2 Lemon, 1 jigger Raspberry Syrup and 1 jigger Brandy. Fill with chilled Champagne and serve.

Gin and Tonic
Place 2 jiggers Dry Gin in a highball glass with 2 or 3 cubes of ice and 1 slice of Lemon. Fill with Tonic Water.

Gin Buck
Place the Juice of 1/2 Lime and 2 twists of Lime Peel in a highball glass with 2 jiggers Gin and ice cubes. Fill up with Ginger Ale.

Golden Lemonade
1 Jigger Eau de Vie de Danzig
1 Jigger Amer Picon
1 Egg Yolk
1 Tablespoon Powdered Sugar
Juice of 2 Limes
Shake well with cracked ice and strain into glass. Fill with chilled Soda Water.

Highballs
Place in a 10-ounce glass ice cubes and 1 or 2 jiggers of any of the liquors listed below. Fill up with Soda Water or plain Water and, if desired, garnish with twist of Lemon Peel.
Applejack
Bourbon
Brandy
Gin
Irish Whiskey
Rum
Rye Whiskey
Scotch Whisky

Note: Occasionally such Wines as Dubonnet, etc. are used to make highballs in the same manner.

Lemonade (Plain)
Juice of ½ Lemon
Juice of ½ Lime
2 Tablespoons Powdered Sugar
Shake well with ice and strain into tall glass. Add extra ice if desired and fill with chilled Soda Water. All Lemon Juice or all Lime Juice may be used instead of half and half. And to vary the drink, Grenadine or other similar sweetening may be used instead of Sugar. Sometimes an Egg is shaken with the mixture. Or, again, the Plain Lemonade is occasionally served with a CLARET FLOAT. (See Floats.)

Macka
Fill a tumbler or highball glass ½ full with cracked ice. Add 1 dash Crème de Cassis and ⅓ each Gin and Sweet and Dry Vermouth. Stir well. Add slice of Orange and serve.

Major Bailey (see Juleps)

Mamie Taylor
In a large tumbler or highball glass, with ice cubes, place 1 slice of Lemon, 2 jiggers Gin or Scotch Whisky and fill with Ginger Ale. Stir and serve.

Modern Lemonade
1 Jigger Sherry
1 Jigger Sloe Gin
2 Tablespoons Powdered Sugar
Juice of 1 Lemon
Stir well with ice and strain into glass. Add twist of Lemon Peel and fill with chilled Soda Water.

Mojito
1⅓ Jiggers Puerto Rican Rum
½ Lime
1 Teaspoon Sugar
Mint Leaves
Squeeze Lime into 10-ounce glass and drop in Rind. Add other ingredients and fill ⅔ full with shaved ice. Add Soda Water, stir and serve.

Moscow Mule
Squeeze into a 12-ounce glass ½ Lime and drop in the Rind. Add ice cubes and 1½ jiggers Vodka and fill with Ginger Beer. Stir and serve.

O'Hearn Special
2 Jiggers Brandy
1 Twist Orange Peel
2 Sprigs Mint
Place in tall glass with ice cubes. Fill up with Ginger Ale. Stir and serve.

Pineapple Lemonade
1 Jigger Brandy
1 Dash Raspberry Syrup
1 Teaspoon Powdered Sugar
2 Slices Pineapple
Muddle the Pineapple and Sugar well in a shaker. Add other ingredients and shake well with ice. Strain into glass and decorate with twist of Lemon Peel and Pineapple Stick if desired.

Pompier
2 Jiggers French Vermouth
⅔ Jigger Crème de Cassis
Place in highball glass with ice cubes and fill up with Soda Water.

Shandy Gaff
Fill tall glass half and half with chilled Ale and Ginger Ale.

Spritzer
Place 2 jiggers White Wine in highball glass with ice cubes and fill with Soda Water.

Stone Fence No. 2
2 Jiggers Scotch Whisky
½ Teaspoon Sugar
1 Cube of Ice

Place in tumbler or highball glass and fill with chilled Soda Water. Stir and serve.

Swedish Highball
2 Jiggers Swedish Punch
1 Dash Bitters
Place in highball glass with ice cubes and fill up with chilled Soda Water.

Tomate
Place in a tumbler or highball glass with ice cubes 2 dashes Pernod and 1 teaspoon Grenadine. Fill with plain Water as desired.

Vermouth Cassis (see Pompier)

PUFFS

All Puffs are served in small tumblers.

Brandy Puff
Place 1 or 2 ice cubes in a glass and add 1 or 2 jiggers Brandy and 1 or 2 jiggers Milk. Fill with chilled Soda Water, stir gently and serve.

Note: The GIN, RUM OR WHISKEY PUFF is made the same as above, substituting the desired liquor.

PUNCHES AND EGGNOGS

American Punch
2 Jiggers White Crème de Menthe
1 Jigger Crème d'Yvette
1 Dash Grenadine
1 Tablespoon Powdered Sugar
Juice of 1 Lemon
Place Sugar and Lemon Juice in bottom of tall glass and dissolve with a little Soda Water. Add Grenadine and fill with cracked ice. Float Liqueurs on top, keeping them separate. Decorate with fruit as desired. Serves 1.

Applejack Punch
2 Quarts Applejack
4 Jiggers Grenadine
1 Pint Orange Juice
Combine the ingredients in a punch bowl with a block of ice. Just before serving add 2 quarts chilled Ginger Ale. Decorate with fruit if desired. Makes 25 to 30 cups.

Artillery Punch
1 Quart Strong Black Tea
1 Quart Rye Whiskey
1 Bottle Red Wine
1 Pint Jamaica Rum
½ Pint Dry Gin
½ Pint Brandy
1 Jigger Benedictine
1 Pint Orange Juice
½ Pint Lemon Juice
Combine all ingredients in a large punch bowl with a block of ice. If found too dry, Sugar Syrup may be added. Decorate with twists of Lemon Peel. Makes 25 to 30 cups.

Bacardi Punch
Fill a tall glass with shaved ice. Pour in ½ jigger Grenadine and 2 jiggers Bacardi Rum. Stir until glass is frosted and decorate with fruit. Serves 1.

Baccio (for 8)
Combine in a large punch bowl with a block of ice 5 jiggers Grapefruit Juice, 5 jiggers Dry Gin, 2 jiggers Anisette, and slices of Orange and Lemon. Add a little Sugar Syrup to taste. Just before serving pour in 1 split chilled Soda Water and 1 split chilled Champagne. Stir slightly.

Baltimore Eggnog
Separate the Whites and Yolks of 12 Eggs. Beat with the Egg Yolks 1 pound Powdered Sugar. Stir in slowly 1 pint Brandy, ½ pint Light Rum, ½ pint Peach Brandy, 3 pints Milk and 1 pint Heavy Cream. Chill thoroughly and fold in stiffly beaten Egg Whites before serving. Makes 25 to 30 cups.

Basic Eggnog (for 1)
Combine in a shaker with ice 2 jiggers Brandy or Light Rum, 1 Egg, 1 tablespoon Sugar and ¾ cup Milk. Shake well and strain into glass. Sprinkle with Nutmeg.

Best Punch
1 Cup Strong Tea
Juice of 2 Lemons
1 Teaspoon Sugar
2 Jiggers Brandy
1 Jigger Curaçao
1 Jigger Medford Rum

Place a large block of ice in a punch bowl. Add the above ingredients. Just before serving, add 1 quart chilled Soda Water and 1 quart chilled Champagne. Makes 10 to 12 cups.

Bombay Punch (2 gallons)
Combine in a mixing bowl, without ice, 1 quart Brandy, 1 quart Sherry, ¼ pint Maraschino, ½ Orange Curaçao and 2 quarts chilled Soda Water. Set punch bowl in a bed of crushed ice, decorate with fruits as desired, and just before serving add 4 quarts chilled Champagne.

Bourbon Eggnog (for 12)
Beat Yolks and Whites of 8 Eggs separately, adding ½ pound Sugar to the Whites. Combine beaten Yolks and Whites and blend gently. Stir in 2 jiggers Rum and 1 bottle Bourbon, 1 pint heavy Cream and 1 quart Milk. Mix all together and chill thoroughly. Serve with grated Nutmeg on top.

Bowle (for 15–20)
(Strawberry, Peach, Pineapple, Orange or Raspberry.)
Strawberry (Erdbeer Bowle)— 1 pint Strawberries, washed and hulled.
Peach (Pfirsich Bowle)—4 ripe Peaches, peeled and halved.
Pineapple (Ananas Bowle)— 2 cups diced, fresh Pineapple.
Orange (Apfelsinen Bowle)—3 Oranges, peeled and sectioned, plus grated Rind of one.

Raspberry (Himbeer Bowle)—
1 pint Raspberries, washed and
picked over.
Put Fruit in punch bowl with
¼ cup Sugar. Place bowl in
refrigerator for a couple of hours.
When ready to serve pour in
3 bottles chilled Rhine or Moselle
Wine and 1 bottle Sekt (German
Sparkling Wine) or other
Champagne, or a quart of Club
Soda.

Brandy Eggnog
Prepare same as BOURBON
EGGNOG, using Brandy.

Brandy Punch
(As served by Patrick Gavin
Duffy to the members of the
Sothern Company during
rehearsals at the old Lyceum
Theatre.)
Juice of 15 Lemons
Juice of 4 Oranges
1¼ Pounds Powdered Sugar
½ Pint Curaçao
1 or 2 Jiggers Grenadine
2 Quarts Brandy
Place in punch bowl with large
block of ice and just before
serving add 1 or 2 quarts Soda
Water. Makes 25 to 30 cups.

Breakfast Eggnog
1 Fresh Egg
¾ Jigger Brandy
¼ Jigger Curaçao
¼ Glass Milk
Shake well with ice and strain
into tall glass. Grate Nutmeg on
top.

Bride's Bowl (for 20)
Dice 2 cups Fresh Pineapple and
place in a punch bowl with ½ cup
Sugar Syrup, 1 cup Lemon Juice,
1½ cups Unsweetened Pineapple
Juice, 1⅓ cups Peach Brandy
and 1½ or 2 bottles Medium
Rum. Add block of ice and before
serving pour in 2 quarts chilled
Soda Water and 1 pint sliced
Strawberries.

Buddha Punch (for 10)
¼ Quart Rhine Wine
4 Jiggers Orange Juice
4 Jiggers Lemon Juice
2 Jiggers Curaçao
2 Jiggers Medium Rum
1 Dash Angostura Bitters
Combine in punch bowl with
block of ice and just before
serving add 1 bottle chilled Soda
Water and 1 bottle chilled
Champagne. Garnish with twists
of Lemon Peel and Mint Leaves.

Burgundy Punch (for 15)
Combine in a punch bowl with a
block of ice 2 quarts Burgundy,
5 jiggers Port, 3 jiggers Cherry
Brandy, Juice of 3 Lemons, Juice
of 6 Oranges, 1 or 2 tablespoons
Sugar and a long twist each
Lemon and Orange Peel. Just
before serving add 2 bottles
chilled Soda Water.

Cardinal (1½ gallons)
Place 1½ pounds Sugar in a
punch bowl and dissolve with 2
quarts Soda Water. Add 2 quarts
Claret, 1 pint Brandy, 1 pint
Rum, 1 jigger Sweet Vermouth,

1 sliced Orange and 2 or 3 slices Fresh Pineapple. Stir and add block of ice. Just before serving add 1 pint of any Sparkling White Wine.

Christmas Punch No. 2
(50 drinks)

In a large punch bowl combine 1 quart strong Tea with a bottle each Rum, Rye Whiskey and Brandy, ½ bottle Benedictine, 1 tablespoon Angostura Bitters and 1 sliced Pineapple. Add the Juice of 12 Oranges, ½ or 1 pound Sugar, dissolved in Water, and mix together thoroughly. Add block of ice and just before serving pour in 2 quarts of chilled Champagne.

Claret Punch No. 1

Fill a tall glass ½ full of cracked ice. Add 1 teaspoon each Lemon Juice, Grenadine and Curaçao. Fill with Claret or Burgundy and decorate with slice of Orange. Serve with a straw.

Claret Punch No. 2

Mix together 2 bottles Claret, ¼ pound Sugar, the Rind of 1 Lemon and chill for several hours. Place block of ice in a punch bowl, pour in the iced mixture. Add 1½ jiggers Cognac, 1½ jiggers Curaçao and 1½ jiggers Sherry. Before serving pour in 2 bottles chilled Soda Water. Makes 25 to 30 cups.

Colonial Tea Punch

Remove the Peel in thin strips from 12 Lemons and place the strips in a punch bowl. Add 1 quart strong Tea and the Juice from the Lemons. Mix with 2 cups Sugar and let stand for 1 hour. Add 1 quart Dark Rum and 1 jigger Brandy. Pour the mixture over crushed ice and serve. Makes 12 to 15 cups.

Curaçao Punch

Place in a large glass ½ teaspoon Sugar, the Juice of ½ Lemon, 1 jigger Curaçao and 1 jigger Brandy or Rum. Fill with shaved ice and stir lightly. Decorate with fruit if desired and serve with a straw.

Dragoon (see Champagne)

Dubonnet Party Punch

Pour 1 bottle Dubonnet into a large pitcher and add 1 pint Gin, the Juice and Rind of 6 Limes and 1 bottle of chilled Soda Water. Fill tall glasses with crushed ice and decorate with Mint. Pour in the Punch. Makes 15 to 20 glasses.

Fish House Punch No. 1 (for 25)

Dissolve ¾ pound Sugar in a large punch bowl with a little Water. When entirely dissolved stir in 1 quart Lemon Juice, 2 quarts Jamaica Rum, 2 quarts Water and add Peach Brandy to taste. Place 1 large block of ice in punch bowl and allow mixture to chill 2 hours. Serve in punch or cocktail glasses.

Fish House Punch No. 2
(the best)
Dissolve in a punch bowl 1½ cups Sugar in 1 cup Water and 3 cups Lemon Juice. Add 3 pints Dry White Wine, 1 bottle Jamaica Rum, 1 bottle Gold Label Rum, 1 bottle Cognac and 2½ jiggers Peach Brandy. Let the mixture stand for 2 or 3 hours, stirring it occasionally. Before serving add a block of ice, stir to cool and serve. If a stronger Punch is desired do not add the block of ice to the punch bowl but set the bowl in a bed of crushed ice to chill.

Gin Punch No. 1
Place in a tall glass 1 lump Sugar, 1 twist Lemon Peel, Juice of ½ Lemon, 2 dashes Maraschino and 2 jiggers Dry Gin. Add cracked ice and fill with Soda Water. Stir and serve.

Gin Punch No. 2 (for 12)
Combine the Juice of 12 Lemons, the Juice of 20 Oranges, 2 quarts Gin, 4 jiggers Grenadine. Pour over large block of ice. Add 2 bottles chilled Soda Water. Decorate with fruit as desired and serve.

Instant Eggnog
Place 2 quarts French Vanilla Ice Cream in a punch bowl. Add 1 Bottle Bourbon and 2 jiggers Jamaica Rum. Stir until creamy and sprinkle with Nutmeg.

Ladies' Punch
Combine in a shaker 2 tablespoons Powdered Sugar, 1 Egg, ½ jigger Maraschino, 1 jigger Crème de Cacao, 1 twist Orange Peel, 1 cup Milk, 2 dashes Nutmeg. Shake well with ice and strain into glass. Serve with additional Nutmeg on top.

Milk Punch (Basic)
Note: The following recipe may be used for Applejack, Bourbon, Brandy, Rum, Rye or Scotch Whisky.
Combine in a shaker with cracked ice 1 or 2 jiggers any liquor desired and 1 cup Milk, 1 tablespoon Powdered Sugar. Shake well and strain into glass. Sprinkle each serving with Nutmeg.

Myrtle Bank Punch
Combine in shaker with a large piece of ice 1 jigger Demerara Rum, 151 Proof, Juice of ½ Lime, 6 dashes Grenadine and 1 teaspoon Sugar. Shake and pour over cracked ice in a 10-ounce glass. Float Maraschino Liqueur on top.

Navy Punch (for 10)
Slice 4 Pineapples and sprinkle well with 1 pound fine sugar. Add ½ bottle Dark Rum, ½ bottle Cognac, ½ bottle Peach Brandy and the Juice of 4 Lemons. Chill well. Pour into punch bowl with block of ice. Decorate with fruit as desired and add 4 quarts of chilled Champagne.

Nourmahal Punch

Squeeze ½ Lime and drop it into a 10-ounce glass with cracked ice. Add 2 jiggers Redheart Rum, 2 dashes Angostura Bitters and fill with Soda Water.

Nuremburg (for 15)

Place ¾ pound lump Sugar in a large bowl and strain over it through a fine sieve the Juice of 2 or 3 large Oranges. Add twists of the Peel cut very thin and pour in 1 quart boiling Water, ⅓ quart Arrack, 1 bottle of Red Wine, which has been heated but not boiled. Stir all together and let cool. Pour into tall glasses over cracked ice.

Note: The mixed ingredients may be bottled. They improve with age.

Patrick Gavin Duffy's Punch

Combine in a shaker with ice 2 jiggers Brandy, 1 jigger Benedictine, ½ teaspoon Powdered Sugar, Juice of 1 Orange. Shake well and pour into tall glass. Decorate with Mint and fruit if desired. Serve with a straw.

Pendennis Eggnog

Mix together 1 pound Powdered Sugar and 1 bottle Bourbon. Let stand for 2 hours. Separate 12 Eggs and beat the Yolks to a froth, adding the Sweetened Whiskey slowly. Let this stand for 2 hours. Whip 2 quarts Heavy Cream until stiff and whip the Egg Whites. Fold these

separately into the Whiskey mixture and chill. This is one of the richest of all Eggnogs.

Pineapple Punch (for 10)

1½ Quarts Moselle Wine
Juice of 3 Lemons
5 Dashes Angostura Bitters
2½ Jiggers English Gin
⅔ Jigger Pine Syrup
⅔ Jigger Grenadine
⅔ Jigger Maraschino
Pour all together into punch bowl with 1 quart chilled Soda Water. Set bowl in bed of crushed ice to chill. Decorate with Pineapple.

Pisco Punch

In a large Wineglass or small tumbler place 1 piece of ice with a teaspoon each of Pineapple and Lemon Juice. Add 2 jiggers Brandy, a small cube of Pineapple and fill with cold Water. Stir well and serve.

Plantation Punch

Combine in a large Old-Fashioned glass 1 jigger Southern Comfort, ½ jigger Lemon Juice, ½ Jigger Rum, 1 teaspoon Sugar. Fill with ice and little Soda Water. Garnish with twist of Orange Peel and serve.

Quintet

3 Jiggers Brandy
3 Jiggers Dark Rum
4 Bottles White Wine
Juice of 8 Lemons
Juice of 8 Oranges

Combine in punch bowl with block of ice and fruit garnish as desired. Just before serving pour in 4 bottles chilled Soda Water. Serves 50 to 60.

Regent Punch (for 10)

2½ Jiggers Brandy
2½ Jiggers Swedish Punch
1¼ Jiggers Curaçao
1 Pint Jamaica Rum
Juice of 6 Lemons
1 Cup Strong Tea
1 Teaspoon Angostura Bitters
1½ Quarts Champagne
Combine all the ingredients except the Champagne in a punch bowl set in a bed of crushed ice. Just before serving, pour in the Champagne and garnish with fruit as desired.

Rhine Wine Punch

3 Quarts Rhine Wine
1 Quart Chilled Soda Water
2½ Jiggers Brandy
2½ Jiggers Maraschino
1 Cup Strong Tea
½ Pound Powdered Sugar
Combine all the ingredients in a punch bowl set in a bed of crushed ice. Decorate with fruit as desired and serve when thoroughly chilled. Makes 25 to 30 cups.

Roman Punch (for 10)

2½ Jiggers Brandy
2½ Jiggers Swedish Punch
1¼ Jiggers Curaçao
1 Pint Jamaica Rum
Juice of 6 Lemons
1½ Quarts Chilled Champagne

1 Teaspoon Angostura or Orange Bitters
1 Cup Strong Tea
Combine all the ingredients in a punch bowl set in a bed of crushed ice. Garnish with fruit as desired and serve when thoroughly chilled. Framboise may be used instead of the Curaçao.

Rum Cow

1 Jigger Puerto Rican Rum
2 Drops Vanilla
1 Pinch Nutmeg
1 Dash Angostura Bitters
1 Cup Milk
2 Teaspoons Sugar
Shake well with ice and pour into a tall glass. This is a specific for morning qualms.

Rum Eggnog

Prepare same as BRANDY EGGNOG, using Jamaica Rum.

Rum Punch (for a large party)

10 Bottles White Wine
2 Pounds Brown Sugar
2 Quarts Orange Juice
1 Quart Lemon Juice
10 Sliced Bananas
2 Fresh Pineapples, cut or chopped
Place the Fruit Juice, Rinds, Bananas, Pineapple and Wine in a crock with the Sugar. Cover and let stand overnight. In the morning add 6 bottles Light Rum and 1 bottle Jamaica Rum and 1 bottle Crème de Banane. Let stand until just before the party.

Strain into punch bowl with ice as needed. Taste for seasoning and add either Sugar Syrup or Lemon Juice as you desire.

Rye Whiskey Punch
Shake with plenty of chopped ice 1 teaspoon Lemon Juice, 2 teaspoons Sugar and 2 jiggers Rye Whiskey. Pour unstrained into 10-ounce glass and decorate with slice of Orange.

Sauterne Punch
Fill a 10-ounce glass ½ full of cracked ice. Add ½ teaspoon Sugar, Juice of ½ Lemon, 1 or 2 teaspoons Curaçao and fill with Sauterne. Stir and decorate with fruit as desired. Serve with a straw.

Sauterne Punch No. 2 (for 10)
½ Pound Powdered Sugar
2 or 3 Quarts Sauterne
2½ Jiggers Maraschino
2½ Jiggers Curaçao
2½ Jiggers Grand Marnier
Combine all together in a punch bowl with a large block of ice. Add several long twists of Lemon and Orange Peel and Mint if desired. Serve when well chilled.

Scotch Whisky Punch (for 12)
Combine in a pitcher with cracked ice 1 quart Scotch Whisky, the Juice and Rind of 3 Lemons, ½ cup Sugar and 1 quart Soda Water. Stir and pour into goblets with extra ice and garnish with fruit as desired.

Strawberry Punch
Place ½ teaspoon Sugar in a 10-ounce glass. Add a little Water to dissolve, and the Juice of ½ Lemon and 1 or 2 teaspoons Strawberry Syrup. Fill ⅔ with shaved ice and pour in 2 jiggers Brandy. Stir and decorate with Strawberries. Serve with a spoon and straw.

Whiskey Punch
Place a block of ice in a punch bowl and pour over it the Juice of 6 Lemons, the Juice of 8 Oranges, 2 tablespoons Sugar and 2 jiggers Curaçao. Stir and pour in 1½ or 2 bottles of Rye, Bourbon or Blended Whiskey. Add fruits as desired and 2 quarts chilled Soda Water. Stir and serve.
Note: 1 quart of iced Tea may be substituted for 1 quart of Soda Water.

Xalapa Punch
Place the grated Peel of 2 Lemons in a punch bowl and pour over it 2½ quarts strong hot Black Tea. Let this stand for 10 or 15 minutes and add 1 pint Sugar Syrup. Let cool. When cold add 1 bottle Applejack, 1 bottle Cuban Rum and 1 bottle Red Wine. Just before serving add a block of ice and 1 Lemon, sliced thin. Serve when well chilled.

Young People's Punch
Combine in a punch bowl ½ pint Sugar Syrup, ½ pint Lemon Juice, 1 pint Orange Juice, 2½ jiggers Curaçao, 2½ jiggers Pineapple Juice, 1½ jiggers Maraschino and 2 bottles Red Wine. Chill with a block of ice and just before serving add 2 quarts of Soda Water. This Punch is excellent when spiked with Brandy as your judgment dictates.

RICKEYS

Basic Rickey
Most Rickeys are made by the following recipe, using 1 or 2 jiggers of Applejack, Bourbon, Gin, Rum, or Whiskey as desired: Place 1 cube of ice in a medium tumbler and add ½ Lime or ¼ Lemon lightly squeezed. Pour in the amount and type of liquor desired and fill with chilled Soda Water. Serve with the Lime or Lemon rind in the glass.

Hugo Rickey
Make the same as GIN RICKEY with 2 dashes Grenadine and 1 slice Pineapple added.

Porto Rico Rickey
Make the same as GIN RICKEY with 2 dashes Raspberry Syrup added.

Savoy Hotel Rickey
Make the same as GIN RICKEY with 4 dashes Grenadine added.

SANGAREES

A Sangaree is always served in a tumbler which may be either small or large, depending on the ingredients used. Regardless of size, it will always have a grating of Nutmeg.

Ale, Porter or Stout Sangaree
Place in a large tumbler ½ teaspoon Sugar dissolved in a little Water. Fill with chilled Ale, Porter or Stout, stir very slightly and serve with a sprinkling of Nutmeg.

Brandy Sangaree
Place in a small tumbler ½ teaspoon Sugar dissolved in a little Water. Add 1 jigger Brandy and ice. Stir and serve with a sprinkling of Nutmeg.
Note: GIN, PORT, RUM, SHERRY, and WHISKEY SANGAREES are all made in this same manner.

SANGRÍA

This immensely popular drink may be made from any reasonably dry Red Wine (and some people are now using dry White). Orginally, Spanish Rioja was the Wine.
1 Bottle Red (or White)Wine

Juice of 2 Oranges
Juice of 1 Lemon
¼ Cup Sugar
2 Jiggers Brandy
Mix well. Add fruit rinds to pitcher. Chill well or add ice.

SCAFFAS

SCAFFAS are served unchilled, undiluted, in cocktail glasses.

Brandy Scaffa
Place in a cocktail glass 1 dash Angostura Bitters and ½ each Maraschino and Brandy. Stir and serve.

Gin Scaffa
Place in a cocktail glass 1 dash Angostura Bitters and ½ each Benedictine and Gin. Stir and serve.

Rum Scaffa
Place in a cocktail glass 1 dash Angostura Bitters and ½ each Benedictine and Rum. Stir and serve.

Whiskey Scaffa
Place in a cocktail glass 1 dash Angostura Bitters and ½ each Benedictine and Bourbon or Rye Whiskey. (A blend will do.) Stir and serve.

SHRUBS

Shrubs may be served either hot or cold but almost always from a large pitcher. And when cold, with plenty of Ice and a fruit garnish.

Brandy Shrub
To the thin Peels of 2 Lemons and the juice of 5, add 2 quarts of Brandy. Cover and let stand for 3 days, then add 1 quart Sherry and 2 pounds Loaf Sugar. Stir well and strain through a fine sieve. Bottle and cork tightly.

Currant Shrub
Boil gently for 10 minutes 2 cups Sugar with 1 pint of strained Currant Juice, skimming frequently. Let cool and when lukewarm add 1 cup Brandy for each pint of the Shrub. Bottle and cork tightly.

Rum Shrub
Combine in a crock 3 pints Orange Juice and 1 pound Loaf Sugar to each 4 quarts of Rum. Cover well and leave for 6 weeks. Then strain, bottle and cork tightly.

White Currant Shrub
Combine 2 quarts of strained White Currant Juice with 4 quarts Rum and 2 pounds Loaf Sugar. Stir till the Sugar is dissolved, cover and let stand for several days. Strain and bottle. Cork tightly.

SLINGS

Brandy Sling
Place in a highball glass 3 cubes of Ice, 1 dash Angostura Bitters, the Juice of ½ Lemon, 1 teaspoon Sugar and 2 jiggers Brandy. Fill with plain Water, stir well and serve.

Gin Sling
Place 1 teaspoon Sugar in a highball glass with 2 jiggers Dry Gin and several cubes of Ice. Fill with Water, stir well and serve. Soda may also be used.
Note: GIN SLINGS may be served hot; if so, sprinkle with a little Nutmeg.

Singapore Gin Sling
Combine in a shaker 1⅓ jiggers
Dry Gin, ⅔ jigger Cherry
Brandy, 1 teaspoon Sugar, Juice
of ½ Lemon and 1 dash
Angostura Bitters. Shake well
with ice and strain into a tall
glass. Add Ice and Soda as
desired. Twist Lemon Peel over
top and garnish with Fruit or
Mint as desired. A dash of
Benedictine may be added.

Straits Sling (for 6)
8 Jiggers Dry Gin
2 Jiggers Benedictine
2 Jiggers Cherry Brandy
Juice of 2 Lemons
1 Teaspoon Angostura Bitters
1 Teaspoon Orange Bitters
Shake well with Ice and strain
into glasses. Fill with chilled
Soda Water as desired and
garnish with fruit.

Vodka Sling
Prepare same as GIN SLING
above.

SMASHES

SMASHES are nothing more than
junior-size Juleps. They are
served in small tumblers, or
Old-Fashioned glasses.

Basic Recipe
Place 1 scant teaspoon fine grain
Sugar in a glass with 2 sprigs
fresh Mint and a few drops of
Water. Crush the Mint with a
muddler and fill glass half full of
shaved ice. Pour in 1 or 2 jiggers
of the desired liquor and if
wanted a squirt of Soda Water.
Decorate with Mint and serve.
Note: Brandy, Gin, Rum or any
Whiskey may be used for this.

TODDIES

TODDIES, when served cold, are all
made the same way whether
Applejack, Brandy, Gin, Rum or
any Whiskey is used.
Place in a small tumbler or
Old-Fashioned glass 1 scant
teaspoon Sugar. Dissolve with a
little Water and leave the spoon
in glass. Add 1 or 2 cubes of Ice
and 2 jiggers of the desired
Liquor. Stir and serve.

ZOOMS

Rum Zoom
Dissolve in a cup 1 teaspoon
Honey in a little boiling Water.
Pour into a shaker with 1
teaspoon Cream and 2 jiggers
Rum. Add ice and shake well and
strain into glass.
Note: BRANDY, GIN and
WHISKEY ZOOMS are all made as
above.

WINE

Wine is a very old beverage but due to a combination of such happenstances as Prohibition, the Anglo-Saxon background of the nation and a greater interest in effect than in nicety, in America wine has lingered in the wings—until recently. Now, it is very much on the march and its rate of increase is the highest among all drinkables.

The Founding Fathers knew their Madeira well (they say G. Washington was a two-bottle-a-day man). T. Jefferson's sojourn in France as our ambassador resulted in the introduction of table wines to the United States. The planting of the vineyards of California with the Vinifera grape of Europe, and the interest of the East in our own native grapes (Labrusca) and, more recently, the so-called French hybrids, have also contributed to a new interest in wine. To the restaurateur and liquor store wine has meant a source of new sales and an extra profit-maker. While we still have a long way to go to catch up with the annual per capita consumption of wine in France and Italy and Argentina of about thirty gallons per person, as compared to our bare one, wine is on the move and interest in it is growing at a remarkable rate.

The prime movers in this are the young people. In a revolt against their parents' cocktail party psychology, and pursuant to their inexpensive charter safaris to Europe where they suddenly find themselves in the wine-twice-a-day world and like it, the twenties to forties are drinking wine and demanding it at home and in the restaurant. Interestingly, they are teaching their seniors to "go and do likewise."

KINDS OF WINE

All wine is the result of the effect of yeast on the sugars in grape juice. The enzymes of yeast attack these sugars in a manifestation called fermentation, converting them to alcohol and CO_2 gas. The gas dissipates (except in Champagne and other sparkling wines) and the grape juice has been converted to wine of one sort or another.

There are basically four types of wine:

TABLE WINE

These are by definition, wines drunk at table with food. They are made by crushing the grapes, fermenting the juice, fining and filtering the wine, aging it and bottling. Nothing is added or subtracted (except in certain instances where chaptalization or sugaring the "must" to result in more alcohol from the fermenting, is permitted). This is the largest category of wine by far. Fourteen per cent is the top in alcoholic strength. Usually table wines are 10 per cent to 13 per cent.

FORTIFIED WINES

These are the stronger (19 per cent to 21 per cent alcohol) wines— the Sherries, Ports, Madeiras, etc. which are not natural but which have grape brandy added to bring up the strength. They are before, after or between meal wines.

FLAVORED WINES

The best known of these is Vermouth, although there are others. They are simply normal wines in which barks and berries, roots and other secret flavorings have been steeped.

SPARKLING WINES

These wines, of which the best known by far is Champagne, are effervescent due to the capture of CO_2 gas within the bottle during a second induced fermentation. The original and unique process, the Méthode Champènoise is complicated, laborious and expensive. Other methods including Charmat (or Bulk) and Transfer, involving pressurized tanks, and even simple Carbonation, are also employed.

Wines can also be differentiated by color—red, white (which means the range from nearly water-white to dark yellow), and pink (which runs the gamut from palest dawn to nearly red). Few realize that red grapes (the majority) can produce red wines (if the skins are left in the vat with the crush twenty-four hours or more); pink wines (if the skins are removed before twenty-four hours); and white (if the skins are removed immediately after crushing). All the pigmentation and most of the tannin is in the grape skins.

Another categorization is according to sugar content or sweetness. The white wines show the greatest contrasts in this, ranging from ultra dry (not sweet) to sweet. The classic example is the difference between a white Graves and a Sauternes. Made from the identical grapes, the former is dry while the latter is sweet (or liquoreux, as the French call it) due to unfermented sugar in the wine, the result of the special late-picked "noble rot" method of producing true Sauternes. Other white wines encompass the spectrum from sweet to dry. Red wines do not show such a broad palate, especially in natural table wines. Among the fortified wines, brandy added during fermentation will stop the process and leave unfermented sugar to sweeten the wine.

AMERICAN WINES

American wines can be roughly divided between California (and Oregon) wines made from the Vinifera grape of Europe and the eastern wines of New York, Pennsylvania, Ohio, etc. made from native (Labrusca) grapes and the relatively new hybrids which endeavor to combine the hardiness of our wild grapes and the more subtle wine producing attributes of the European vines.

California. There are basically three broad categories of West Coast wines: 1. The Varietals; 2. The Generics; 3. The Monopoles or trade-marked, proprietary products.

Varietals are wines given the name of the grapes from which they are made. This is permitted when 51 per cent of the wine in the bottle is from this grape. The other 49 per cent is within the discretion of the maker. Varietals are, basically, America's best wines and the costliest. Some names to look for are Cabernet Sauvignon (counterpart of a red Bordeaux or Claret); Pinot Noir (counterpart of a red Burgundy); Pinot Chardonnay or simply Chardonnay (counterpart of a white Burgundy), Semillon (counterpart of a white Graves); Zinfandel (a true American now though of European origin—the origin having been lost), Riesling or Johannisberg Riesling (counterpart of a Rhine, Moselle or Alsatian).

Generics parrot the European place names the wines seek to emulate; Burgundy, Claret, Sauternes, Champagne, Chianti, Rhine. Some are more successful at the charade than others. There is no legal requirement as to content.

Monopoles or *Proprietaries* are produced by just one maker in contradistinction to the many who produce competing Varietals and/or Generics. If you want a Paisano, only Gallo makes it. Should you opt for Emerald Dry, only Masson makes that. They are the secret and special product of the manufacturer and they are uniquely his own.

There are so many producers in California these days, it would be well-nigh impossible to list even a representative selection. A few are huge producers of inexpensive wines, and do not cross into the Varietal world at all. Others are large producers who straddle the tripartite divisions of wine types, making some of each. There are still others, some quite large and some so small as to earn the sobriquet, "boutique," which confine their production to Varietal wines only. Prices follow the above break-down in ascending order—the lowest prices being for the Generics (except Champagne) and Proprietaries, and the highest tags for the smaller-production Varietals. When it is realized that a ton of first quality, high-demand "noble" grapes approaches the $1,000 price mark, and that a ton of ordinary, common (often table-type) grapes goes for $100 or thereabouts, it is perhaps understandable that the range both in quality and price is very wide indeed among California wines (which represent 70 per cent plus of all the wines we drink).

In the eastern U.S.A. the situation is quite different. The grapes are different. The producers are fewer (though Taylor in New York is the counterpart of Gallo in California, in being the volume juggernaut). The problems are different. The product is different.

Severe winters of the East (and when we say East, we mean New York in particular though many other eastern states are in the act, to a greater or lesser degree) make raising the vinifera family almost impossible. Of recent years, Konstantin Frank and Charles Fournier (of Gold Seal) and a few other hardy souls have shown that selected vinifera can be grown and can be made into very respectable wine. However the vast bulk of eastern wine depends upon such storied American names as Concord, Niagara, Scuppernong, Delaware, etc. These were bearing when Lief the Lucky sailed our shores down to "Vineland," the name he gave Newfoundland from his Scandinavian lair. Many eastern producers prefer to market these grapes under proprietary names and a very large percentage (much larger proportionately than in California) have chosen to market their wine in the guise of sparkling wine—New York or Ohio Champagne. The most recent development has been the enormous interest shown in the so-called French hybrids, one-time Baltimore *Sun* publisher Philip Wagner being a leader of this hybridizing venture, whereby the hardy qualities of Labrusca rootstock are married to the better wine-producing propensities of the Vinifera vine. The result has been a compendium of new grapes known by number and/or hybridizar (Seibel, Foch, etc.). A few have been found worthy of their own wine names such as Chelois, Baco Noir, etc.

In summing up the American scene, this can be said: enormous strides have been made, both west and east, in the forty years since Prohibition ended. The U.S. wines can do us proud. To say the Westerners are the exact counterparts of their European forebears, or that the eastern hybrids are either, would be carrying chauvinism too far. To say they are somewhat different is not to say they are inferior. After all, vines planted six thousand miles from whence they came, in foreign soil with other and various weather conditions and sun intensities, could hardly be expected to duplicate their native achievements. I think it is all to the good that we have disparate taste experiences to regale us—and all hail to the men who have made it possible in such a short time and against such odds.

FRENCH WINES

France is, of course, the pre-eminent example of wine-making although, in certain years, Italy produces a greater quantity. Spain, Portugal, Germany (and to a lesser degree Hungary, Yugoslavia, Switzerland, Austria, Bulgaria and Romania) have gotten into the export act, and the U.S.S.R. hovers in the wings.

The three great wines of France are Bordeaux, Burgundies and Champagnes—followed by the wines of the Loire, the Rhône, Alsace, Provence and a host of lesser areas.

BORDEAUX

Unquestionably the greatest wine area in the world, producing vast quantities of wine (500,000,000 bottles per annum or better), both red and white. What distinguishes Bordeaux is that the cream— that is, the better wines as compared to the total ouput—is thicker in Bordeaux than anywhere else in the world. There is no one who hasn't heard of the great Chateaux—such names as Ch. d'Yquem, Ch.

Lafite, Ch. Mouton-Rothschild, Ch. Margaux, Ch. Latour, Ch. Haut-Brion, Ch. Pétrus, Ch. Ausone, Ch. Cheval Blanc and the like. But there are many, many other Châteaux, one hundred or so "Classified" and hence elect, and thousands of "petite" or lesser ones.

A "Château" wine is made from the grapes *of* a single property, *on* that property, but there are many fine regional wines which are blends of wine from grapes grown in smaller or larger areas—from "Bordeaux," to "St. Émilion" or "St. Estèphe" or "Entre-Deux-Mers," blended from grapes grown within the confines of the geographic area carefully delineated on the label.

This might be as good a place as any to explain the rigorous system of quality control set up by France for the protection of the consumer—the so-called "Appellation Controlée" laws. Most of the wines we see bear these words on the label, separated by a geographic designation; viz. Graves, or Burgundy or Rhône or Médoc or whatever is appropriate to the wine.

Additionally, aside from geography, the words imply that the wine is made from the kind of grapes permitted for that type of wine; that the process used in making is the approved one for the wine in question; and finally, that the wine produced from any vineyard represented in the bottle has not exceeded the maximum gallonage set by law for production on that property.

No other nation has such strict accountability although Americans have promulgated some binding rules and regulations, and Italy is trending toward a similar codification, as is Germany—and perhaps other countries with whose laws I am not acquainted.

BURGUNDY

Burgundy is second to Bordeaux only in quantity, producing about one third the Bordelaise gallonage. The wines of Burgundy, red and white, can be very fine indeed. The noble reds are well-known; the whites are *among,* if not *the,* greatest in the world. They are dry. There is no gradation from dry to sweet as in Bordeaux. "Estate-bottled" is a similar designation to the "Château" designation in Bordeaux; a village wine, such as Aloxe-Corton (Aloxe, the town; Corton its most famous vineyard name, which is allowed as a designation for all the vineyards of the area about Corton); Gévrey-Chambertin (Gévrey, the town; Chambertin the prime vineyard—and so on). Corton, Chambertin, Musigny, Richebourg, Bonnes-Mares, Nuits-St.-Georges, Grands Echézaux, Romanée-Conti—these are some of the greatest red Burgundies; Montrachet, Corton-Charlemagne, Chevalier and Bâtard Montrachet, Meursault, Chablis, are some of the greatest whites.

Probably the most interesting distinction between Bordeaux and Burgundy is that in the former, a Château wine is *one* thing, made by *one* proprietor, no matter from whom or where you buy it. In Burgundy, contrariwise, a vineyard may have a plethora of owners—over fifty for Clos de Vougeot for example. Now, every one doesn't make his own wine (though he would be entitled to). He delegates his grapes to another owner, and so does his neighbor and *his* neighbor. Even so, eight or ten Clos de Vougeots, all of the same vintage, is a commonplace. That is why, in Burgundy, the shipper (or négotiant, who buys and bottles the wine) is so all-important. His name on the bottle is what counts. There are many fine shippers, and Burgundy drinkers (or buyers) should learn some of them as they would their ABCs.

Beaujolais, so very popular and so very sought after in the U.S.A. is not really a Burgundy. However, it is grown in a nearby area and is a Burgundy by definition but is made of the Gamay, not the Pinot Noir grape. However, it is the favorite of many Americans—easy to say, easy to drink, and not demanding such long aging. In fact, drinking "nouveau" or "primeur" (the wine of the year of the vintage) Beaujolais is quite the "in" thing.

RHÔNE

A large volume of wine, of varying quality and availability, is grown within the watershed of the great river. Most of it is red.

The best known is America's darling—Châteauneuf-du-Pape, named for vineyards of the Popes when they lived in Avignon. When Châteauneuf is good it is very, very good, and when it is bad, it is—you know! Most of it is in between. The better names to seek out are Hermitage and, above all, Côte Roti.

The majority of the wines are red— a few white, such as Hermitage Blanc, are available and one great rarity, Château Grillet. This vineyard, once the property of Charlemagne, of about three and one half acres, produces three hundred and fifty U.S. gallons a year, total.

One of the Rhônes great claims to fame is its rosé, Tavel. Tavel was the first, and still perhaps the best, of the pink wines. Gigondas is another good one—this one red, and Condrieu, dry and semi-sweet and wonderfully perfumed.

LOIRE

This lovely river purls through Châteaux and vineyards. If it never gave us anything but Pouilly-Fumé and Sancerre, that would be enough—but Vouvray is the principal wine: dry, sweet, still and sparkling, and sometimes very good. Bourgueil and Chinon are quite excellent reds, made from the Cabernet Franc. Quincy is another name worth knowing. When the Loire reaches Brittany, it waters the vineyards of Muscadet, Brittany's only "appellation controlée" wine— dry and perfect with shellfish.

ALSACE

Alsace is an extension of the German Rhine and Moselle. Its wines are similar—all white though more highly perfumed. All are 100 per cent of the grape from which they are made. I think Riesling is the best though the most distinctive is Gewürtztraminer (made from a clone of the Traminer grape), spicy and fruity. Syvaner is a peg below. Get to know the shippers in Alsace—they count heavily.

CHAMPAGNE

Who needs to be told about this, the queen of sparkling wines? To France and most of the world (Japan, England, Spain and Canada have recently fallen into line) only the wines of the de- marcated Marne area, Champagne, may be called Champagne and then only if made from the red Pinot Noir and the white Chardonnay and Pinot Meunier, and made by the Méthode Champènoise. That means a blending (cuvée) of wines from red and white grapes, a secondary fermentation induced in the bottle; a long period under temporary cork; extraction of spent yeasts by freezing the neck and "remuage"; a "dosage" to make up for lost wine; and a long rest. Expensive? You bet. Worth it? Yes.

In the United States, "Champagnes" can be from other grapes and made by pressure tank, bottle transfer, and carbonation. The label must say so—and also where the wines come from; viz. Cali- fornia, New York, Ohio, etc.

ETC.

There are plenty of other wines made in France, coming from the Jura, Saumur, Provence, Corbière, Languedoc etc. Some are excellent; all are worth exploring.

Not all—few in fact—of these are "appellation" wines. Some are VDQS (Vin Délimité de Qualité Supérieure), a second rung. Some are not indicated by either designation. Drink them as "vins de pays" or "vins ordinaires," the wines for everyday drinking.

ITALIAN WINES

Italy makes an enormous quantity of wine mostly for home consumption.

The best wines come from the North: Lombardy, Tuscany, Piedmont, Veneto.

Probably the most famous wine of Italy is Chianti but the straw-covered bottle of old has pretty much disappeared overseas. Today, "Classico" Chiantis are shipped in regular "Bordeaux" bottles. These are from special "Classico" vineyard areas. The neck label will identify. The rooster is the ⚹1 and most usually seen. Other devices, such as the "putto" or little angel, a bunch of grapes, a Roman ruin, etc. mark above average chiantis.

Probably Barolo is Italy's top wine—this from Piedmont, along with Barbaresco. Gattinary, Barbera, Grignolino are also from this area. From Lombardy, watch for Grumello, Sassella, Inferno; from Veneto, white Soave and red Valpolicella and Bardolino.

Orvieto from Umbria, Verdicchio from the Marches and Corvo from Sicily are excellent whites. Marsala is a dessert wine, deservedly famous. Asti Spumante is Italy's sparkling wine.

Of late, tougher laws are keeping Italian wines on an escalating ladder of excellence.

SPANISH WINES

Sherry—a fortified wine from Jerez—made by blending wines of various years and types, and strengthening with grape brandy—has dominated Spanish wine production.

But, of late, Spanish Rioja (and a derivative, Sangría, made by adding fruit juices) has come into its own. Riojas vary but at their best resemble a French Bordeaux, and take on age gracefully.

PORTUGUESE WINES

The pink wines of Portugal have taken America by storm: Mateus, Lancers and others are among the largest-selling and most popular wines extant. Easy drinkin'—easy pricin' does it.

OTHER EUROPEAN COUNTRIES

Switzerland's red Dôle and white Fendant, Neuchâtel and Aigle; Austria's white Gumpoldskirchner and Loibner Kaiserwein; Hungary's Eger's Bikavér (red), Badacsonyi (white) and Tokays (white); Greece's St. Helena; Yugoslav Dingač and Greek Zilavka (white); Turkish Buzbağ, Bulgarian Muscatel (white) and Greek Mavrodaphne (red) are just a few of Europe's other wines worth seeking out and assaying.

OTHER COUNTRIES

Australia, New Zealand, Chile and Argentina are a few other countries for the wine buff to explore. The first two are popular in the mother country but appearing here now. Chile's wines have long been known for excellence at a minimum price. Argentina, a huge wine producer and consumer, is only lately sparing a bit for us—both reds and whites (from the Mendoza area) and the price is right!

STORING WINE

In general, wines like a temperature between 55 and 60°. Five°, more or less, will not damage them. The main precaution is not to subject them to constant or abrupt changes in temperature. The storage problem is usually simple for restaurateurs and home owners who have cool cellars, but difficult for apartment dwellers who live in rooms kept at 70° or higher. Better not attempt to store large amounts of wine if the temperature is not right.

Store both natural and sparkling wines on their sides so that liquid keeps the cork wet. If the cork dries out, air seeps in and spoils natural oil; or gas escapes from Champagne, which then turns "flat." Fortified wines and liquors can sit upright. So can most California wines.

SERVING WINE

People enjoy wine because it looks good, smells good, tastes good. The ideal wineglass enhances this trio of sensations. The glass is clear; it is large enough so the wine can be swirled and "sniffed"; and it is a convenient shape for drinking. Through the years, certain wines have become associated with certain sorts of glasses, but present-day usage encourages the "all-purpose" glass: tulip-shaped, with a capacity of about 8 ounces. Such glasses are available nearly everywhere. In pouring wine, fill the glasses only ⅓ to ½ full.

Serve the following wines chilled: all white wines; Champagne and other sparkling wines; rosé wines; dry Sherries and Madeiras. Do not chill until the wine is icy cold for this kills its flavor. About 45 to 50° is right. You can bring the wine to this temperature by refrigerating it for an hour or so, or by chilling it in a wine cooler 15 to 20 minutes.

Serve the following at room temperature: all red wines, except Beaujolais, which, if you wish, can be chilled slightly; Port, and the sweeter Madeiras and Sherries. Red wine should be opened about an hour before serving and permitted to "breathe"—this improves its bouquet.

Wine baskets are an affectation. They were invented to help servants move great Burgundies from the cellar without stirring up the sediment. If you have sedimented wines, decant them about an hour before serving. Or simply handle the bottle carefully. White wines seldom contain sediment, and to decant a white wine or to carry it in a basket is silly.

VINTAGE

There is nothing wrong with using a Vintage Chart to guide you through the labyrinth of wines and dates. But there is something very wrong in using it as you would the multiplication table; 7×6 is always 42 but a 5 in such a chart as this may range upward to 6 or 7 or down to 3 or 4. It depends on the kind of wine, the producer, the shipper, how it's been kept, etc. So, if you don't play the numbers too seriously, the chart will be of help.

Read it as running from 10 (best) to 0 (worst), remembering the above admonitions and being constantly mindful that wine is alive in the bottle and is always changing.

Blank spaces mean no vintage or NV.

Valuations of older white wines (except long-lived ausleses, spätleses or oddities) are for what they were—not what they are. Many, over 4 or 5 years of age, are probably well over-the-hill. This book will hopefully have a long life so that any evaluation on publication must be reassessed as the years go on.

To simplify a few things:

1959—pretty nearly all wines excellent

1961—one of the century's greatest wine years

1963–1965–1968—the poorest of the decade of the 60s. Fun for the explorer.

1962–1964–1966—decent wines, generally speaking

1967—quite decent; light in Bordeaux

1969—fairly good

1970–1971—bode fair to be excellent years, especially 1970

1972—sometimey

1973—shaping up quite well

Average life:		
Champagne	10 years
White Bordeaux, Alsace, and Loire	5 to 6 years
White Burgundy and Rhone	8 years
Rhine and Moselle	4 years (except late-picked and specially selected)
Red Bordeaux	20 to 50 years
Red Burgundy and Rhone	10 to 25 years
California White	2 to 4 years
California Red	5 to 20 years
Italian White	2 to 4 years
Italian Red	5 to 15 years

VINTAGE CHART

	1959	1960	1961	1962	1963	1964	1965	1966
Burgundy—Red	10	7	10	8	4	8	3	8
Burgundy—White	9	5	10	8	5	6	5	7
Bordeaux—Red	10	6	10	8	4	8	3	8
Bordeaux—White	10	6	10	6	4	7 dry 5 sweet	4	7 dry 5 sweet
Rhône	9	6	9	7	3	7	3	8
Loire	10	5	9	8	4	8	2	7
Alsace	10	5	8	7	5	8	1	7
Champagne	10		9	8		8		9
Rhine and Moselle	9		8	6	4	8	6	8

	1967	1968	1969	1970	1971	1972	1973
Burgundy—Red	7	2	6	9	8½	7	7
Burgundy—White	6	5	8	8	9	7	7
Bordeaux—Red	7½	2	5	9	6	6	7
Bordeaux—White	6	4	7	9	8	6	6
Rhône	7	2	6	10	10	9	9
Loire	7	5	9	9	9	8	7
Alsace	9	2	7	8	10	9	8
Champagne	8		8	9	8		7
Rhine and Moselle	9	3	9	7	10	6	8

TRADITIONAL AFFINITIES
BETWEEN FOOD AND WINE

These are suggestions, not rules. Most people like the combinations listed, but your personal preference should make the decision. Restaurateurs and people who entertain large groups find it best to adhere to the traditional affinities rather than to experiment. They can be sure that time-tested combinations of food and wine will please nearly everybody.

Champagne is congenial with food throughout meals. As an appetizer, serve *Brut;* serve *Brut* or *Extra Dry* up to dessert; serve the sweeter Champagnes only as dessert wines.

Food	*Domestic Wine*	*Imported Wine*
Appetizers, snacks, hors d'oeuvres	Dry Sherry, Rosé Wines	Dry Sherry, Dry Madeira
		Rosé Wines
		Chablis
		Muscadet
		Dry Rhines and Moselles
		Dry Italian Whites
		Italian Vermouth, Iced
Oysters on the half shell		Chablis, Muscadet
Soup	Medium Sherry	Medium Sherry
		Madeira (not too sweet)
Shellfish, fish dishes, cold chicken and turkey	Dry Semillon Johannisberg Riesling Riesling Pinot Blanc Chardonnay Sauvignon Blanc Folle Blanche Sylvaner	Chablis and other white Burgundies: Meursault Montrachet Pouilly-Fuissé Muscadet Grâves, Entre-Deux-Mers Dry Rhines and Moselles

	Traminer Native Whites	Dry Italian Whites Alsatian Wines
Salmon	Dry Whites, as above Rosé Wines	Dry Whites, as above Rosé Wines Beaujolais
Roasts and chops (except pork and veal), pot roasts, liver	Cabernet, Zinfandel and other Light Reds Barbera	Red Bordeaux Red Burgundy
Veal roasts and chops	Dry Whites	Dry Whites
Pork roasts and chops	Dry Whites Rosé Wines	Dry Whites Rosé Wines Champagne
Roast ham	Beer Rosé Wines	Beer Rosé Wines
Full-flavored red meats, all game, including venison and duck	Pinot Noir Gamay Burgundy	Red Burgundies Red Rhône Wines Red Chianti Barolo Barbera
Salad bowls	Riesling and other light Dry Whites	Alsatian Dry Rhines and Moselles
Nuts	All the robust Reds suggested for meat and game Port Sweeter Sherries	All the robust Reds suggested for meat and game Port Sweeter Sherries

CHEESE

| Fresh Cheeses
Farmer
Cream
Cottage | Rosé | Rosé |

Soft Cheeses Brie, Camembert, etc.	Cabernet Pinot Noir Zinfandel	Clarets Burgundy
Double and Triple Crêmes	Riesling Sauvignon Blanc	Graves Rhine Moselle Alsatian
Hard Cheeses Cheddar, Edam, Cheshire, etc.		Any good dry red or white wine—or Beer.
Desserts	Sweet Semillon California Sauterne	Sweet Rhine Wines Sauternes
Coffee	Brandies and Liqueurs Sweeter Sherries Port	Cognac and Liqueurs Sweeter Sherries Madeira Port

DISPENSING DRAUGHT BEER*

There is probably no beverage as sensitive to mishandling as draught beer. Yet three simple fundamental principles control the many details involved in the proper dispensing of perfect "brewery fresh" draught beer. These are *proper refrigeration, cleanliness* and *proper pressures.*

Since draught beer is perishable, it must not be exposed to warm temperatures. The retailer must preserve it by providing equipment that will maintain the temperature of the beer in the barrel between 38°–42° F. These temperatures should be maintained throughout the dispensing equipment so that the beer in the glass as it is served to the consumer will be at 38°–42° F. This range of temperature seems to satisfy the majority of tastes and is too small a variation to affect its flavor or quality.

Cleanliness is a most vital consideration. The beer faucets, tubing, hose, coils, taps, and vents, including direct draw systems, must be throughly cleaned at regular intervals. Glasses must be immaculate and sparklingly clean. No effort should be spared to keep the bar

* Prepared by Anheuser-Busch, Inc.

clean and bright. Odors and appearances that might be disagreeable must be avoided.

Proper pressure in the barrel is very important. To maintain "brewery fresh" taste in the beer, its natural or normal carbonation must be preserved. The dispensing equipment through which the beer flows must have a pressure that corresponds to the normal carbonation of the beer at the temperature of the beer in the barrel. The size and length of the coil in the dispensing equipment will determine the pressure to be used.

With the dispensing equipment properly set up, the retailer is ready to serve draught beer. To draw beer, hold the glass at an angle close to the lip of the faucet—open the faucet all the way—lower and straighten up the glass as the beer flows into it so that the desired foam is formed—about one-half inch before the glass is full close the faucet all the way. The foam will rise to the top of the glass, completely filling it without overflowing. A desirable glass of draught beer should include about 20 per cent foam.

BEERS

Half and Half (American Style)
Fill glass half full of Beer and fill up with Porter.

Half and Half ('Alf and 'Alf) (English Style)
Fill glass half full of Beer and fill up with Ale.

FOOD TO GO WITH DRINKS

The problem of what food to serve with drinks is easy to solve these days. The markets offer an abundance of wonderful delicacies. There are so many appetizing things that can be made up easily for a cocktail party that no one should ever have to resort to the old potato chip and salted peanut routine. Nor should anyone feel compelled to offer the dits and doots popular a few years ago. Trays of tired sections of bread with colored cream cheese and odd designs are actually not very appealing to most people. Besides, such dits and doots require far too much preparation. My advice is to take it easy. Serve simple, substantial appetizers.

Here are a few of the simplest things to serve with drinks. Most of them can be held in reserve on the shelf or in the refrigerator. Nearly all can be readied quickly when friends and neighbors drop by for drinks.

NUTS

You may buy salted nuts of all kinds in tins. They keep fresh for a long time. The peanut, of course, is the standby, but other varieties are even better and more original as accompaniments to drinks.

Try **Macadamia nuts** from Hawaii with a taste rather like a hot biscuit; **fava beans,** roasted (not really a nut but in the same category); **chick peas,** toasted and salted—very crisp and with a most distinctive flavor; **pistachio nuts**—the large white, salted ones are the best; **walnuts**—these delectable nuts, toasted and salted, are too often neglected; **Mexican sunflower seeds**—crisp and well salted; **giant pecans,** toasted and well salted.

It is no trick to salt your own almonds and filberts and the difference in price is astonishing. Oregon filberts, in particular, are unusual and tasty cocktail bits if treated correctly. Here are a few ideas for preparing nuts that can be eaten warm or stored in glass jars.

SALTED ALMONDS IN THEIR COATS

Spread 1 pound of shelled almonds in their skins in a large, flat baking pan or cookie sheet. Sprinkle with salt to taste and dot lightly with butter. Bake at 350° for 25–35 minutes, or until the nuts are nicely toasted but not charred in flavor. Taste often after the first 25 minutes and be on the alert for the prize moment. Remove the nuts, and let them cool on absorbent paper.

VARIATIONS

Blanched Almonds: Place the nuts in boiling water for 2–3 minutes to loosen the skins. Slip the skins off with the fingers. Place the blanched almonds in a baking pan or sheet and add 4 tablespoons butter or ⅓ cup oil. Toast in the oven at 350° until nicely browned and crisp. Sprinkle with salt to taste and drain on absorbent paper.

Garlic Almonds: Proceed as in either of the recipes above but add Spice Islands garlic seasoning powder to the nuts before putting them in the oven. Or blend 2 cloves of finely chopped fresh garlic with ⅓ cup oil and pour over the nuts before roasting. Salt to taste when you remove the nuts from the oven.

Curried Almonds: Add 1 tablespoon curry powder to the mixture above and swirl the nuts around in it as they roast.

Chili Almonds: Substitute good chili powder for curry and mix well with the nuts.

SALTED FILBERTS OR PECANS

Place filberts in flat baking pan with salt and butter or oil. Toast at 350° for 25–35 minutes. Drain on absorbent paper.

Garlic or Curry Filberts: Place 1 pound pecan halves in a flat baking pan. Dot with butter and sprinkle with salt. Bake at 350° for 20 minutes or until the nuts are toasted and crisp. Drain on absorbent paper.

Garlic or **Curry** or **Chili Pecans:** Add seasonings as above.

SALTED PEANUTS

Proceed as with salted pecans.

DUNKS AND DIPS

The dunk is practically an indoor sport. A bowl of one or two different mixtures with raw vegetables, potato chips or tiny codfish balls enhances almost any sort of gathering. Dunks are made with a mayonnaise or sour cream base, and some have cream cheese or cottage cheese added for body.

HERB DUNK FOR RAW VEGETABLES

Combine 1½ pints of sour cream with 1 teaspoon salt or more; 1 cup chopped spinach; ½ cup each chopped parsley, chives and dill and 1 clove garlic, chopped fine. Blend thoroughly and let chill for 2 hours before serving.

VARIATIONS

Mustard: Omit the dill and add 2 tablespoons French mustard and 1 teaspoon dry mustard to the mixture.

Pungent: Omit dill and add ¼ cup chopped green pepper, ½ cup chopped cucumber and 1 tablespoon chili powder and 1 teaspoon freshly ground black pepper.

Anchovy: Add 1 can anchovy fillets, chopped fine, a hard-boiled egg, chopped fine, and 1 teaspoon orégano. Omit the dill. Add 3 tablespoons capers.

Tart: Add ¼ cup chopped pickled onions and 4 tablespoons capers to the basic mix, omitting the dill. Add 3 tablespoons lemon juice and some freshly ground black pepper.

VEGETABLES FOR DUNKING

Any raw vegetable, crisp and cold, goes with these sauces. Some of the less usual ones are tiny *raw asparagus tips* (once tasted they make you wonder why you have eaten only cooked asparagus all these years) ; the *finger* or *seedless avocado,* now becoming more popular and plentiful; *Chinese water chestnuts,* speared with a toothpick, excellent because of their delightful crispness.

The regulars are *carrots, green onions, cauliflower flowerets, turnips, radishes* (including the *Japanese radish* cut in slices), *zucchini, cucumber fingers, cherry* or *plum tomatoes, celery, anise, fennel,* and *endive stalks.* All very pleasant to munch with cocktails.

DIPS FOR SHRIMP AND OTHER SHELLFISH OR CHICKEN OR TURKEY FINGERS

These are suitable for vegetables but are primarily for sea food.

SHRIMP DIP

Combine 2 cups mayonnaise with ½ cup chili sauce, 1 tablespoon anchovy paste, ½ cup chopped green onions, 2 hard-boiled eggs, chopped rather fine, ¼ cup parsley, chopped fine, salt and pepper to taste.

PLAIN DIP

It's hard to surpass a fine mayonnaise made from good olive oil, egg yolks, salt, pepper, mustard and lemon juice. Perfect with shrimp or lobster or with any fish on toothpicks.

ORIENTAL DIP

Combine 1 cup mayonnaise, 1 cup sour cream, 2 tablespoons chopped ginger, 1 tablespoon soy sauce, 2 tablespoons chopped water chestnuts, 2 cloves of garlic, chopped fine, ½ cup chopped green onions, 1 tablespoon chopped Chinese parsley (cilantro or fresh coriander) if available, ¼ cup chopped parsley. This is elegant with either shrimp or lobster.

SPREADS

This is another easy approach to entertaining. Arrange a big bowl of spread surrounded by thinly sliced and buttered (or not buttered, as you will) rye bread, pumpernickel, lavish in pieces, cracker bread, fine protein bread—any selection of good breads and crackers.

CHEESE SPREADS

Liederkranz, Liptauer, Maroilles, etc., cheeses should be selected carefully. They should be soft but not runny and have a good ripe flavor. Mash them with a fork, adding 2 tablespoons chopped chives, ¼ cup chopped parsley, 3 tablespoons capers, 1 teaspoon dry mustard, 1 tablespoon Worcestershire sauce and about ¼ cup sour cream. Beat well, taste for seasoning and let the mixture ripen for an hour or two before serving. Sprinkle with paprika and chopped parsley before serving. If the spread seems thin, fold in a little cream cheese to give it body. Many people, in place of making a spread, use Boursin, Boursault, and other spicy cheeses just as they come.

CRABMEAT SPREAD

Combine 1 pound or 2 cans crabmeat with 1 seeded and shredded cucumber, ¼ cup chopped parsley, ¼ cup chopped green onions and ½ cup mayonnaise. Season with lemon juice and ¼ cup of rum. Let stand 2 hours and drain. Arrange in a bowl and sprinkle with chopped parsley.

AVOCADO SPREAD OR POOR MAN'S BUTTER

Mash 3 very ripe avocados and add ½ cup chopped green onions, 1 teaspoon salt, 1 teaspoon chili powder and 2 tablespoons chili sauce.

Blend well by hand or in the electric mixer. Sprinkle lavishly with chopped parsley. Good as a spread with toasted tortillas or with carnitas.

RAW MEAT SPREAD

This is an all-time favorite with drinks. Combine 1½ pounds ground round steak with no fat (have it freshly ground), 1 egg, 1 teaspoon dry mustard, 1 tablespoon French mustard, 2 tablespoons A-1 sauce, ½ cup chopped green onions, 1 clove garlic, cut fine. Blend well and place in a large bowl and sprinkle with chopped green onions and parsley. Serve with generous amounts of pumpernickel and hot toast.

ROQUEFORT CHEESE SPREAD

Combine 1 pound Roquefort cheese with ½ pound cream cheese, ¼ pound butter, 1 teaspoon freshly ground black pepper, 1 teaspoon dry mustard, 3 tablespoons Worcestershire sauce and ¼ cup Cognac. Beat well until the mixture is well blended. Refrigerate in small jars. This is an excellent cheese course at dinner.

LANGLOIS BLUE VEIN CHEESE SPREAD

Langlois cheese is one of the great achievements of American cheese-making. Here is a recipe from Mrs. Hansen, head of the Langlois firm:

Combine 1 pound Langlois blue with an equal quantity of cream cheese and 1½ cups chopped walnuts. Moisten with a little Cognac. Cream it well and store in small jars.

HELEN BROWN'S IN-A-MINUTE CHEESE SPREAD

This is based on a cheese mixture called Whiz, which is to be found almost everywhere. Combine it with A-1 sauce, Worcestershire, mustard, chili powder or sauce, or with chopped green onions and salt and pepper. Serve with crackers or pumpernickel. Easy, good and very quick.

CHEESE BALLS

Combine 1 pound cream cheese with 1 pound cottage cheese, 2 tablespoons each chopped green onions and parsley and 1 cup chopped nuts. Season with salt and pepper and dry mustard. Form into small balls, roll in chopped parsley or chopped nuts, and chill for a half hour or so. Serve impaled on toothpicks.

HOT PARMESAN DELIGHTS

This recipe was perfected by the food consultant to the Taylor Wine Company, in Hammondsport, New York. It is simple and tasty.

Combine 1 cup mayonnaise, ½ cup grated Parmesan cheese, 2 teaspoons Worcestershire sauce, dash of onion seasoning or 1 tablespoon chopped green onions. Add 1½ tablespoons Sherry or Cognac and blend well. Spread on toast squares or on crackers, and sprinkle with a little additional cheese. Brown under the broiler and serve very hot.

APPETIZERS

Sausage Balls (makes about 50)

This is a popular recipe, especially down South.

In a large mixing bowl put 1 pound pork breakfast sausage meat, 1½ cups grated Cheddar cheese, 1½ cups flour, 1 teaspoon salt, ½ teaspoon pepper. Work well together. Roll out little marbles (¾″) with your floured hands. Spread balls on a cookie sheet. Put in your freezer compartment until frozen solid. Transfer to Baggies and leave in freezer until needed. Then bake as many as you wish (3 a person is average) in a 350° oven for 25 minutes. Let cool and stand 10 minutes to crisp. Serve on toothpicks.

Cheese "Things" (makes 3 dozen)

Combine 1¼ cups butter (soft), 2 cups flour, 2 cups grated cheese (Cheddar or similar), salt and pepper. Roll into a large sausage, 3″ or so in diameter. Wrap and place in freezer and keep frozen. When ready to use, slice off ⅛″ thick slices. Put on cookie sheets. Bake about 15 minutes at 375°.

Quiche Lorraine (Serves 6–8)

In a mixing bowl, work 1½ cups flour, ½ teaspoon salt, ¼ pound soft butter, 2½ tablespoons water. Make into ball. Chill for an hour. Roll dough out thin and line 10″ pie plate or quiche tin. Refrigerate. Cook 1 dozen strips bacon. Drain. Crumble into piecrust. Preheat oven to 400°. Break 4 eggs into bowl. Add 1½ cups cream, salt and pepper to taste, a pinch nutmeg and a pinch sugar. Mix well. Hold. Sprinkle 1 cup grated cheese (¾ Swiss and ¼ Parmesan is best combination) over bacon in crust. Pour in the egg-cream custard. Bake quiche 10 minutes. Then reduce heat to 350° and bake another 20 minutes, or until quiche is nicely browned.

(A variation is to add a cup of red onion, diced and sautéed in butter. Pour over bacon before you add cheese and custard. Some use just the onion and eliminate the cheese.)

PÂTÉS TO BE USED WITH COCKTAILS

HOME-STYLE PÂTÉ

This can be used for cocktail snacks or for sandwiches.

Purchase 1½ pounds lamb's liver, in thin slices, or pork liver; also 1½ pounds ground pork and 1 pound salt pork, cut in thin slices. A good addition is a pound of pork loin cut in paper-thin slices.

Hard boil 4 eggs. Then poach the liver in a skillet with 1 cup wine —red wine or Sherry—1 bay leaf, 1 teaspoon salt, 2 teaspoons freshly ground black pepper, 2 cloves garlic. Let it cook slowly, and if there is not enough wine to cover add a little consommé or stock. When the liver is very soft pull it apart and chop it rather coarse. Combine with the ground pork, 1 teaspoon thyme, 3 garlic cloves, chopped fine, 1 teaspoon dry mustard, ½ cup Sherry or Cognac or whiskey and enough of the broth from the liver to make a fine paste.

Line a casserole or loaf tin with slices of salt pork. Then put down a layer of the meat mixture. Imbed the peeled, hard-boiled eggs in the meat. Sprinkle with chopped green onions and parsley, add a little Cognac or whiskey, then cover with meat mixture. Next make a layer of thinly sliced pieces of pork, sprinkle with chopped green onions and parsley, add a little more Cognac or whiskey and some freshly ground black pepper. Cover again with the mixture and then salt pork slices. Bake covered for 2½ hours at 325°. Take from the oven, remove cover and place a weight on the pâté to cool. When it is cool, remove the weight and store the pâté in refrigerator till ready to use. Slice very thin.

Serve with hot buttered toast, pumpernickel or hot French bread.

QUICK PÂTÉ

Combine 1 pound good liverwurst, ½ pound cream cheese, ½ cup raw mushrooms, chopped fine, 1 garlic clove crushed and chopped and ¼ cup Cognac or whiskey. Beat well together, form into a loaf and serve with toast and buttered thin slices of bread.

BREAD AND SANDWICHES

HOT HERBED BREAD

Split loaves of French bread the long way. Spread with a mixture of ½ cup each chopped green onions, parsley butter with 1 teaspoon salt, 1 teaspoon freshly ground black pepper, and 1 tablespoon fresh or dried tarragon or 1 teaspoon thyme. Press the two pieces together and heat in a 400° oven for 10 to 15 minutes. Cut in 3–4 inch lengths. Serve piping hot with the butter melted well into the bread and the herbs heated through.

SESAME SEED BREAD

Split loaves of French bread in half the long way. Spread with garlic-flavored butter and sprinkle heavily with sesame seeds. Heat in a 400° oven for 10 minutes and brown under the broiler for 3–4 minutes. Cut in 3–4 inch chunks.

CHEESE AND HERB SANDWICH

Split loaves of French bread in halves the long way. Make a paste of ½ pound butter, ½ pound grated Switzerland Swiss cheese, ½ cup chopped green onions, ½ cup chopped parsley. Spread the halves with this mixture and press them together. Heat in a 400° oven for 12–15 minutes or until cheese and butter are melted.

HOT AND PUNGENT CHEESE SANDWICH

Combine ½ pound grated Switzerland Swiss cheese with 1 teaspoon dry mustard, 1 tablespoon curry powder, ½ cup chutney and blend well. Spread split loaves of French bread with the mixture and heat at 400° until the mixture is hot and bubbly and the bread crisp.

INDIVIDUAL HERO SANDWICHES

Split small crisp French rolls in halves the long way. Butter them well. On each roll place a few thin slices of tomato, salami, cheese, licked peppers, anchovies and sliced ripe olives. Press together and cut in halves. These are substantial and excellent for a large party.

THIN SANDWICHES

A well-made sandwich, of thin bread with plenty of butter and filling, is just about the most satisfying cocktail accompaniment.

Use good breads: pumpernickel, rye, thinly sliced white or whole-wheat bread, protein bread. Spread the slices well with unsalted butter and fill lavishly. Cut the crusts from the sandwiches and cut them into fingers—no fancy shapes are necessary. Pack them in foil and store them in the refrigerator for several hours before serving. Or freeze them the week before and thaw just before serving.

Here is a list of fillings that are very successful for cocktail service:
Thin slices of real Virginia ham
Good smoked ham with pungent mustard
Rare roast beef with horseradish butter
Turkey or white meat of chicken with mayonnaise
Thin slices of corned beef or pastrami
Chopped seeded and peeled tomato
Thin slices of cucumber
Thin slices of onion
Thin slices of onion with parsley and mayonnaise
Chopped ripe olives and onions with mayonnaise
Chopped shrimp with curry mayonnaise
Chopped chicken gizzards and hearts with chutney and fresh
   ginger
Chopped gizzards with mayonnaise and chopped green onion
Chopped chicken liver with egg and onion
Chopped anchovies, hard-boiled eggs, green onions, parsley
Chopped olives, pimentos, nuts, garlic, parsley
Thin slices of salami
Thin slices of smoked salmon with cream cheese and onion
Thin slices of smoked sturgeon
Pâté de foie (tinned) on white bread with plenty of butter
Chopped cucumber, tomato, onion, ripe olive
Thin slices of tongue with hot mustard

SMOKED FISH

The pungence of smoked fish provokes thirst. It's a waste of time to cut up bits of fish and serve them on toast. Rather, serve a platter of various kinds with bread and butter, crackers, a little oil and vinegar, capers, a pepper mill and a pile of thinly sliced onions. Among the favorites are paper-thin slices of pink smoked salmon, marble-like slices of smoked sturgeon, whole smoked whitefish, smoked butterfish. Smoked eel is elegant. Smoked tuna and smoked cod are wonderful.

HERRING WITH SOUR CREAM

Chop 6 or 8 fillets of pickled herring rather coarsely—enough to make 2 cups. Combine with 1 cup each of mayonnaise and heavy sour cream. Season with ¼ cup each chopped dill and chopped shallots or green onions. Provide a ladle and plenty of thin rye bread.

CANNED FISH

No matter where you are, you'll find canned smoked fish on the market. Thinly sliced smoked salmon is available, also smoked sturgeon, smoked cod, smoked shad, smoked tuna, smoked eel, salmon in a solid pack. Most come in various sizes. I recommend keeping a stock of canned fish on hand for those occasions when you want to offer a snack and drinks.

Sardines of various kinds, served in the can accompanied by toast and crackers, are another favorite cocktail standby.

A rarity, but worth searching for—brood eels (unborn eels) in olive oil. Just heat with a clove of garlic. Spoon over toast points. Lovely, once you get over the idea.

FOOD FOR A LARGE PARTY

BAKED HAM

A large ham—Virginia, Tennessee or Georgia country ham—is delicious with cocktails. Serve a good-sized one, and be sure there's someone who knows how to carve it in thin, thin pieces across the top. Have bits of thinly cut small French bread and a selection of mustards. The flavor of ham helps to make cocktails more delectable, and there is no waste.

ROAST TURKEY

Turkey has the same good qualities that make a ham so pleasant with drinks. There is no waste and it is better to have some good turkey meat left over than a lot of spreads. Serve it with buttered bread and toast and some good pickles and relish and a bowl of raw vegetables and a good dip.

ROAST BEEF

A large roast of rare beef—just warm, not hot—and slabs of well-buttered and thinly sliced bread are unbeatable for a substantial cocktail snack. Be sure the carver slices the beef as thin as possible, and that you provide good mustard and horseradish with sour cream.

THE THING

This simple "thing" will be consumed by the quart. Children like it, and so do grandparents.

Combine various breakfast cereals: bite-size hunks, oatmeal cereal that comes in tiny rings, the crispies and crunchies that have body. To 2 quarts of the cereal add 1 pound small peanuts, a good sprinkling of Spice Islands garlic seasoning powder, a good sprinkling of chili powder. Salt to taste and dot well with butter. Toast at 300°–325° for 45 minutes to an hour. Shake the pan often and mix well with a spoon or fork so that there is an evenness of browning and crisping and mixing in of flavors. Salt and serve. Store in air-tight containers.

ON YOUR SHELVES

Here's a list of things you can keep on hand for times when you want to have a snack with a drink without too much bother:

Ripe olives or green olives; chill and serve or mix them with a little olive oil and garlic.

Stuffed olives

Cheese biscuits: there are some fabulous Dutch cheese crackers made like puff paste. Heat them and serve.

Anchovies in olive oil. Merely open a good-sized tin and serve with crackers or bread. Lemon should be around.

Sardines of all descriptions

Herring tidbits in tins

Smoked oysters

Tiny cocktail sausages

Tiny cocktail shrimp

Parched corn

INDEX